FIFA World Cup A-Z o

Introduction

The Greatest Show on Earth it ha
every professional footballer's career, it s an ...
aspired to play in when we were young and fresh faced. Ever since the idea was thought up of staging a competition to produce the best team, with the best players in the world, we all pretended to be one of the greats of the game Puskas, Pelé, Charlton, Cruyff, Maradona, Zidane or Messi the list goes on through the years of these magical icons of The FIFA World Cup.

'The FIFA World Cup', these four words make the hair stand up on the back of your neck when the fever of this wonderful spectacle of football pleasure comes around in our lives. The build up to the World Cup is more than just the finals itself; it is the worry and joy of watching your nation during qualification, debate amongst fans if the coach has picked the right team and formation. It is from the elation of your nation qualifying from their group, to the anticipation of wondering which teams your nation will play in the finals. Watching or listening to the endless build-up of the finals draw, doesn't feel tedious or dreary to the World Cup fanatic, this is the one single most important moment in his/her life at that instant. Sit back and enjoy the wonder of ex World Cup stars picking little black balls out of a clear plastic fishbowl and unveiling who on a strip of paper your nation will be playing against…. heaven!

Once the marvel of The Draw is over, the die-hard of us football fans will be working out where on Earth these venues are, and logistics of getting to the finals begin. Or in the case of millions, imagining and predicting the scores of each game prior to the tournament, working out your nation's route to the final, and who they would play on their way there. For the next few months fans of football will be hoping, praying that the elite stars of the game will be fit to play in the ultimate event on the planet.

As soon as it is the date for the tournament to begin, all countries involved and some that are not get into the fever that is The FIFA World Cup. It takes over the supporter's day to day activities, panini sticker swaps are the most important fixation for adults and children alike. Homes are draped in their nation's flags, and wallcharts are up in every room. World Cup fever takes over.

Every occupational job is worked out, so not a ball kicked will be missed, production takes a back seat for a month in factories and corporate jobs. The world stands still, until their team is knocked out, and only then reality comes around again.

The FIFA World Cup began in 1930, a full 26 years after FIFA was formed, before that the only organized world event for football was the Olympics, but this was for amateurs. Jules Rimet the FIFA president decided to make their own tournament in 1928 and took it on himself to make this a reality.

From 1930 there must have been stories of sheer delight, pleasure and enjoyment for fans that had the privilege to see such skill, ability and capability of the legends on show. Also, there must have been tears of frustration, disappointment and distress in defeat. Stories of fans journeys as they strive to get to watch games, they have saved up for the past few years, and the tales that have come their way along their voyage.

My main aim when writing this book was to make a handbook for the fans of football to take with them where ever they were going, a small book that could be put in their coat pocket, and whipped out to read whenever they needed a quick fix of World Cup facts and trivia. I have tried to gather a lot of the stories that have occurred on and off the pitch during the history of the World Cup, some familiar and some not so. Also assembling such details as World Cup firsts and lasts, oldest and youngest, records of individual and team contributions into such a pocket-sized book has been a difficult task, but I have tried to get the main interesting facts that I thought made each World Cup special. Some will make you laugh, some weep and some make you marvel in astonishment. There are curiosities, and sensations in every tournament which makes you admire the phenomenon that is The Greatest Show on Earth.

WORLD CUP 1930

ARGENTINA V URUGUAY

~~4-2~~
2-4

FIFA World Cup A-Z of Facts and Figures

TEAM	PLACING	P	W	D	L	F-A
URUGUAY	CHAMPS	4	4	0	0	15-3
ARGENTINA	RU	5	4	0	1	18-9
USA	SF	3	2	0	1	7-6
YUGOSLAVIA	SF	3	2	0	1	7-7
CHILE	R1	3	2	0	1	5-3
BRAZIL	R1	2	1	0	1	5-2
FRANCE	R1	3	1	0	2	4-3
ROMANIA	R1	2	1	0	1	3-5
PARAGUAY	R1	2	1	0	1	1-3
PERU	R1	2	0	0	2	1-4
BELGIUM	R1	2	0	0	2	0-4
BOLIVIA	R1	2	0	0	2	0-8
MEXICO	R1	3	0	0	3	4-13

FIFA World Cup A-Z of Facts and Figures

A
As holders of the Olympic title and the fact that 1930 marked its 100 years of independence, it was appropriate to choose Uruguay to host the first WORLD CUP tournament.

B
A dispute regarding which country would supply the **ball** for the final was discussed and resolved, rumour has it that for the first half a ball from Uruguay was used and then for the second half Argentina chose one of theirs.

C
The venue of the first ever WORLD CUP Final was the stadium **Centenario**. Even though not being completely finished, having 3 tiers and 2 tiers in some places, but this didn't stop 10 out of the 18 matches, including all three knockout contests, and 2 games in a day being played there. Jules Rimet called it 'a temple of football'. It's still the national stadium today, with an aggressive and merciless atmosphere, as anyone who witnessed the recent play-off battles with Australia will testify.

D
Adalbert **Desu** of Romania has the accolade of scoring the fastest goal of the WORLD CUP tournament after 50 seconds, in their match against Peru. It also had the lowest ever attendance of 300, although the official figure was 2,549. Looking at photographs of the empty stadium, 300 sounds more likely.

E
Every game in the finals had at least one goal scored in it, some as many as eight. One famous missed goal was Vidal of Chile, when his penalty was saved by France's Thepot, this being the first penalty awarded in a WORLD CUP. Also, in this game Alex Villaplane the French captain played his last match. He was later executed in the War for collaborating with the Germans.

FIFA World Cup A-Z of Facts and Figures

F
France met Mexico in the opening match on the 13th July and duly thrashed them 4-1. Lucien Laurent of France scored the first ever World Cup goal after 19 minutes. Manuel and Felipe Rosas of Mexico were the first brothers to play in a WORLD CUP. USA also played Belgium at the same time winning 2-0.

G
The number of **games** totalled at eighteen, and the number of goals scored was an impressive 66. Averaging over 3 goals per game. 4 groups were used, 4 teams in one group, and 3 teams in the others. The winners and runners up in each group would contest the semi-final.

H
Hat-trick confusion. There still seems to be a difference of opinion on who scored the tournament's first ever hat-trick. Whilst FIFA and other sources say USA's Bertram Patenaude scored the first World Cup hat trick (17 July 1930, against Paraguay), others insist it was Guillermo Stabile of Argentina, with three goals two days later against Mexico.

I
The **isolation** of many of the top European teams was due to how far they had to travel. Even though the Uruguayan government was willing to pay expenses, many refused to travel.

J
The **Jules Rimet** trophy or "Victoire aux Ailes d'Or" trophy was made for the winners by Abel Lafleur. A statuette 30cm high made of solid gold and weighing 4 kg, it was a worthy prize to win.

K
King Carol of Romania gave his players three months off from their jobs and a guarantee that they would be re-employed on their return, as well as granting amnesty to suspended players. Oh yes, and he also appointed himself as coach.

L
The referee for the final was a Belgian named John **Langenus**, who was famous for wearing plus-fours.

M
Montevideo was the venue for all the games, with its three stadiums (Centenario, Pocitos and Parque Central). Celebrations in Montevideo went on for several days and nights and the day after the famous victory, the 31 July, was proclaimed a national holiday.

N
Uruguayan captain Jose **Nazassi** was the first man to hold aloft the Jules Rimet trophy.

O
The **organizer** of the inaugural WORLD CUP was one Hugo Meisl, an Austrian who also created The Mitropa Cup, a Central European International Cup.

P
Pablo Dorado has the enviable record of being the first ever scorer in a World Cup Final. Pedro Castro who scored the last goal in the final, had no right hand after he had the misfortune of losing it whilst using an electric saw in his job as a carpenter.

Q
Qualification. For the first ever WORLD CUP there were no qualifying rounds - participation was by invitation only. 12 said yes, the rest is history.

R
Gilberto **Rego**, the referee for Argentina v France blew his whistle for full time 6 minutes early and had to bring the players back on to restart the match. Warnken of Chile lost control of the game Romania v Peru, where a player got his leg broke, and Placido Galindo of Peru got his marching orders; the first player to be sent off in a finals match.

S
Guillermo **Stabile** of Argentina was the tournament's top scorer with 8 goals, thus becoming the first winner of the Golden Shoe/Boot award.

T
Jose **Tramutola** the Argentinian coach was the youngest coach to grace the finals at 27 years 267 days.

U
Uruguay was the first nation to hold the WORLD CUP and its first winners. The first final was contested by the hosts and their neighbours Argentina. After trailing 2-1 at the interval, Uruguay went on to win 4-2 and thus won the cup.

V
The **voyage** to Uruguay from Europe was a lengthy and boring journey. Belgium, France, Yugoslavia and Romania, set sail on 21 June 1930 from Villefranche-Sur-Mer with the liner "Conte Verde" reaching Rio de Janeiro on 29 June, where they picked up the Brazilian squad and arrived in Montevideo on the 4th July.

W
Why no England? Moaning about having to play in the same tournament as countries they went to war against and arguing with FIFA over the definition of 'professional footballer', led to England's footballing wilderness. They wouldn't compete in the competition for another 20 years.

X
Final XI: **Uruguay**: Ballesteros, Naszo (c), Mascherano, Andrade, Gestido, Fernández, **Dorado (12)**, Scarone, **Castro (89)**, **Cea (57)**, **Irearte (68)**
Argentina: Botasso, Della Torre, Paternóster, Evaristo j, Monti, Suárez, **Peucelle (20)**, Varallo, **Stabile (37)**, Ferreira (c), Evaristo M.

Y
Yugoslavia has the distinction of being the first European team to reach the semi-finals., the USA being the other non-South American nation. Both semi-finals were won 6-1.

Z
Zumelzu of Argentina was the first player to score a penalty v Mexico in their 6-3 win.

WORLD CUP 1934

ITALY V CZECHOSLOVAKIA
2-1 aet

FIFA World Cup A-Z of Facts and Figures

TEAM	PLACING	P	W	D	L	F-A
ITALY	CHAMPS	5	4	1	0	12-3
CZECHOSLOVAKIA	RU	4	3	0	1	9-6
GERMANY	SF	4	3	0	1	11-8
AUSTRIA	SF	4	2	0	2	7-7
SPAIN	QF	3*	1	1	1	4-3
HUNGARY	QF	2	1	0	1	5-4
SWITZERLAND	QF	2	1	0	1	5-5
SWEDEN	QF	2	1	0	1	4-4
ARGENTINA	R1	1	0	0	1	2-3
FRANCE	R1	1	0	0	1	2-3
NETHERLANDS	R1	1	0	0	1	2-3
ROMANIA	R1	1	0	0	1	1-2
EGYPT	R1	1	0	0	1	2-4
BRAZIL	R1	1	0	0	1	1-3
BELGIUM	R1	1	0	0	1	2-5

FIFA World Cup A-Z of Facts and Figures

A
Argentina had entered, but their best three players played for Italy. 'As they had Italian origin and were willing to fight and die for Italy in WWI, they were able to play for us', is how coach Pozzo put it. This was known as Oriundi. The Argentinian team was a team of amateurs, with only 1 player previously capped (Devincenzi.) They were knocked out by Sweden 3-2, and wouldn't play another WORLD CUP game till 1957.

B
Brazil who didn't have to qualify (Peru withdrew) and were knocked out at the first hurdle by Spain 3-1, fielding 8 new caps in the game. Leonidas was the only black player in the team.

C
Czechoslovakia the unlucky runners up, were 8 minutes from holding the trophy aloft. An agile, skillful team lost 2-1 in extra time. They got to the final by beating only European teams.

D
Dictator Mussolini paid for all the participating teams' expenses, and even had a cup made for the winners that dwarfed the Jules Rimet Trophy. It was aptly called Coppa Del Duce.

E
England and its stiff upper lip attitude of thinking them above other nations still did not enter because of the boundaries of amateur and professional football.

F
Fewest goals scored to date in this WORLD CUP, equaling 1930's 70 goals.

G
Germany battled their way to third place (first ever) beating neighbouring Austria 3-2 in Naples, where only 8,000 spectators came to watch. Before their game v Sweden, the team gave Nazi salutes towards Mussolini's box. They also came onto games with a

swastika on their flag, ironically their captain Fritz Szepan was of Polish origin.

H
Hugo Meisl the Austrian 'Wunder Team' coach was one of the first coaches to adopt a total footballing philosophy. The Jewish banker took the Austrians to the semis.

I
Italy the tournament favourites and eventual winners were Europe's first host nation. They were also the top scorers in the tournament with 12 goals, 4 of which were scored by Angelo Schiavio, the great Italian forward, who also scored the WORLD CUP'S 100th goal v USA.

J
Joyous captain of the winning team was Luis Monti the roving Italian (Arg) centre half.

K
Knock-out was now in favour, dispensing with group stages from previous tournament. Sixteen teams entered.

L
Lowest average attendance ever for a WORLD CUP of 23,235.

M
Rene **Mercet** was the ref for the Italy v Spain quarter final, and disallowed 2 Spanish goals, and favoured the Italians. Some say that he was 'got at' by the fascist regime; he was later suspended by the Swiss FA.

N
All **Non**-European countries were knocked out in the first round. Teams from South America had travelled 8,000 miles for one match.

FIFA World Cup A-Z of Facts and Figures

O
Oldrich Nejedly of Czechoslovakia was Top Scorer with five goals and was awarded the Bronze Ball for being the 3rd best player in the tournament.

Q
Qualification for the tournament was a first and provided Spain and Hungary as dark horses, and Egypt was represented as the first from the African continent. Even the hosts had to qualify. 32 teams in preliminary round.

R
A **replay** was used for the first time in World Cup history, in the first ever WORLD CUP drawn game Italy v Spain Quarter Final 1-1.

S **Stadium** of the National Fascist Party was the venue of the final in Rome. Both captains in the final were goalkeepers.

T
Edmund Conen became the first **teenager** to score a hat-trick in a WORLD CUP v Belgium in Germany's first game; the score ended 5-2 to Germany.

U
Uruguay 1930 winners declined to defend the trophy on the grounds that most of Europe snubbed their WORLD CUP…. bit petty.

V
Vittorio Pozzo used the sistema formation on the field, using a 2-3-2-3 strategy to create a stronger defence, and was sent by the fascist dictator Mussolini to England to study tactics.

W
Hugo Meisl's **Wunderteam** Austria was the Olympic champions and favourites to win the competition, with their talisman and star player Matthias Sindalar in the team. They would eventually lose 1-0 in the semifinal v Italy. Their game v France was the first WORLD CUP game to go to extra time. Frances' first ever coach was an Englishman

named George KIimpton. Sindalar would tragically take his own life in 1939 by gassing himself.

X
Final **XI**: **Italy:** Combi (c), Monzeglio, Allemandi, Ferraris IV, Monti, Bertolini, Guaita, Meazza, **Schiavio (95)**, Ferrrari, **Orsi (81)**
Czechoslovakia: Planicka (c), Zenizek, Ctyroky, Kostalek, Cambal, Krcil, Junek, Svoboda, Sobotka, Nejedly, **Puc (71)**

Y
Yet again Luisito Monti was in the final. In 1930 it was for Argentina, this time he won it with Italy. First man to play in 2 finals. Italy won it after extra time.

Z
Zamora the Spanish ace keeper performed heroics v Brazil but was injured in the first Quarter-Final game v Italy, and subsequently missed the replay two days later which Spain lost.

WORLD CUP 1938

ITALY V HUNGARY
4-2

FIFA World Cup A-Z of Facts and Figures

TEAM	STANDINGS	P	W	D	L	F-A
ITALY	CHAMPS	4	4	0	0	11-5
HUNGARY	RU	4	3	0	1	15-5
BRAZIL	SF	5"	3	1	1	14-11
SWEDEN	SF	3:	1	0	2	11-9
CZECHOSLOVAKIA	QF	3"	1	1	1	5-3
FRANCE	QF	2	1	0	1	4-4
SWITZERLAND	QF	3*	1	1	1	5-5
CUBA	QF	3*	1	1	1	5-12
ROMANIA	R1	2*	0	1	1	4-5
GERMANY	R1	2*	0	1	1	3-5
POLAND	R1	1	0	0	1	5-6
NORWAY	R1	1	0	0	1	1-2
BELGIUM	R1	1	0	0	1	1-3
NETHERLANDS	R1	1	0	0	1	0-3
DUTCH EAST INDIES	R1	1	0	0	1	0-6

"Replay QF
: Walkover
*Replay R1

FIFA World Cup A-Z of Facts and Figures

A
Austria one of the great football powers, was now no longer a country, swallowed up by the *Anschluss.* They qualified in October, but by April the FA ceased to exist. So, some of the Austrian squad was added to the Germans. Not Matthias Sindelar who now had to wear the Star of David on his clothing.

B
The first player that seems to have played on his **birthday** at the finals was said to be France's Emile Veinante on his 31st v Italy, France lost 3-1. He also scored a goal after 35 seconds v Belgium.

C
Coach Vittorio Pozzo was again the manager, and the only one to win 2 WORLD CUP'S back to back. He also sent his team out v France in an all-black fascist black kit.

D
Dutch East Indies (modern Indonesia) became the first Asian qualifiers. Their captain Nawir was a doctor who played in glasses, and the majority was students. A compromising 6-0 score by the Hungarians ended their only WORLD CUP dream.

E
Still no **England** or Home Nations. England who had won in Germany and France would have been one of the favourites, but the FA turned down an invitation to take Austria's place.

F
France was hosts of the 3rd World Cup, so didn't have to qualify (a first.) Argentina didn't enter the tournament on the grounds that they should have hosted. France won one game, and then lost to Italy in the Quarters. 10 cities hosted the games, the final being played in the Stade Olympique de Colombes.

G
Germany to the delight of Europe was knocked out in the first round after a replay by Switzerland, who refused to give a Nazi salute. They

led the replay 2-0, against 10 men, and still lost 4-2. Shame.

H
Hungary became runners up. Their keeper Szabo misunderstood a message that read *Vincere o morire which* he thought meant Win or die, relieved thinking that he had spared the lives of the Italian players by losing, but the message read Victory or bust, a slogan of encouragement from the fascist era.

I
Italy victorious again, the first team to win back to back World Cups. Only Meazza and Ferrari left from 1934 final. A much more athletic team with pace and fitness kept turning defence into attack throughout the tournament. As previous winners they didn't have to qualify (a first.)

J
Jack Butler became the first English coach at a WORLD CUP. He coached the Belgians, albeit to a 2-1 defeat against the hosts.

K
Keeper with the worst WORLD CUP blunder must be France's Laurent Di Lorto. With an easy looped volley heading towards him, he hopped up for an easy catch then decided to push it away. He then palmed it sideways, tried to follow it as it fell into the net, he crashed into the post, and then kicked the ball away in disgust. All his own doing and he never played for France again.

L
Leonidas da Silva was top scorer with 7 goals. The sturdy little Brazilian with his pencil moustache stood out even more when he started the game v Poland in his socks because of the muddy pitch. The ref Eklind made him put his boots back on.

M
Manager with the distinction of making one of the worst decisions in WORLD CUP history was Pimenta of Brazil. Thinking that they

would easily beat Italy in the Semi's he dropped Leonidas to rest him for the final. Brazil was dually knocked out 2-1.

N
Norway nearly beat Italy in the first round, and ran Italy ragged. A disallowed goal and fine keeping kept Italy in the tournament after extra time, and eventually became the winners.

O
Oldest hat-trick scorer in WORLD CUP history to this date, is Tore Keller from Sweden v Cuba 33 years 159 days, but some sources say it was his teammate Harry Andersson who got the hat-trick.

P
Silvio **Piola** was Italy's star striker: and the best player in Europe at the time; 30 goals in 34 games, he excelled in The Azzuri's use of wingers, especially Biavati, and scored 2 in the final.

Q
Qualification consisted of 37 teams, but only 27 played. The rest withdrew for numerous reasons. Spain was in a Civil war. So, Cuba, Dutch East indies, Brazil and Romania qualified without playing. Poor Latvia who was 2nd in Austria's group was not invited, so only 15 teams were in the finals.

R
Replays were used again, this time three times, but now with more time between games.

S
Sweden got a bye in the 1st round, played Cuba and won 8-0(only WORLD CUP apps) to book a semifinal place v Hungary who hammered them 5-1, but only after Arne Nyberg had scored the then fastest World Cup goal after 35 seconds.

FIFA World Cup A-Z of Facts and Figures

T
The **top** scorers in the tournament with 15 goals were Hungary. They were easily the most exciting going forward, and had 2 formidable strikers in Zsengeller and Sarosi, who netted 10 between them.

U
Underdogs of the tournament Cuba caused an upset by beating Romania after a replay, to become the first WORLD CUP shocks. They then played Sweden 3 days later, probably exhaustion played a part in their 8-0 trouncing. Wetterstrom of Sweden scored 4 that day.

V
Vice-President of FIFA, Dr Torino Barassi, hid the trophy in a shoebox under his bed throughout the Second World War and thus saved it from falling into the hands of occupying troops.

W
Ernest **Wilimowski** of Poland goes in the record books as the first player to score 4 goals in a match (v Brazil), and still be on the losing side 6 goals to 5. He was later press ganged into playing for Germany during the war and scored 13 goals.

X
Final XI Italy: Olivieri, Foni, Rava, Serantoni, Andreolo, Locatelli, Biavati, Meazza ©, **Piola (16, 82),** Ferrari, **Colaussi (6, 35)**
  Hungary: Szabo, Gyula, Polgar, Biro, Szalay, Gyorgy, Szucs, Lazar, Sas, Vincze, **Sorosí © (69),** Zsengaller, **Titkos (7)**

Y
A pair of **Y-fronts** were nearly on display in the Semi's when Meazza who had just scored a penalty, ran to the sidelines to change his shorts. Whilst putting the ball on the spot for the penalty, he bent down and snapped the elastic in his shorts.

Z
Zaniest game of the tournament was between Brazil and Czechoslovakia. This was a war on a football pitch, broken bones for

Planicka and Nejedly, who were out for the replay, 3 sending's off. Planika never played for his country again after this.

WORLD CUP 1950

URUGUAY V BRAZIL
2-1 GROUP GAME

FIFA World Cup A-Z of Facts and Figures

TEAM	STANDINGS	P	W	D	L	F-A
URUGUAY	CHAMPS	4	3	1	0	15-5
BRAZIL	RU	6	4	1	1	22-6
SWEDEN	3RD	5	2	1	2	11-15
SPAIN	4TH	6	3	1	2	10-12
YUGOSLAVIA	R1	3	2	0	1	7-3
SWITZERLAND	R1	3	1	1	1	4-6
ITALY	R1	2	1	0	1	4-3
ENGLAND	R1	3	1	0	2	2-2
CHILE	R1	3	1	0	2	5-6
USA	R1	3	1	0	2	4-8
PARAGUAY	R1	2	0	1	1	2-4
MEXICO	R1	3	0	0	3	2-10
BOLIVIA	R1	1	0	0	1	0-8

FIFA World Cup A-Z of Facts and Figures

A
Rodriguez **Andrade** of Uruguay and his uncle Jose became the first nephew and uncle to win the WORLD CUP; Jose won it with Uruguay in 1930.

B
Brazil top scorers with 22 goals for the tournament were odds on favourites. They beat Sweden 7-1 and Spain 6-1 in the final group games. Every time they scored, the pitch was showered with journalists, for on the spot interviews, still happens today. In those days Brazil played in all white.

C
Antonio **Carbajal** of Mexico started his first of 5 World Cup's in this tournament, a record that jointly stands to this day. The first game of the World Cup, and his first cap v Brazil ended in a 4-0 loss.

D
A **different** captain was used for each of USA's games. Keough v Spain because he spoke Spanish, McIlvenny v England because he was British, and v Chile it was Bahr because he was the real captain.

E
Hooray!!! **England** finally agree to join the World Cup bandwagon, but didn't get through the group stage, losing to the USA 0-1, when wired through to the papers back home, the publishers deemed this must be wrong, and reported it as a 10-1 win. England's first ever finals game was v Chile and won 2-0.

F
A **final** was not catered for, but one materialized all the same, and perhaps the most exciting of all time. Brazil only had to draw v Uruguay to become champions. A crowd of 200,000 somehow cramped into the Maracanã. Overall Brazil had 30 shots at goal, but the Uruguayan defence stood tall, until the start of the second half when Friaca scored his first goal for Brazil. This spurred the Uruguay team on and 20 minutes later was level. Still the Brazilian's went forward and got caught again with just over 10 minutes to go.

FIFA World Cup A-Z of Facts and Figures

G
Gaetjens the Haitian-born American scored the winning goal, and probably produced the most shocking score line in World Cup history. England legends such as Alf Ramsey, Billy Wright, Stan Mortensen, Tom Finney and Wilf Mannion, couldn't find a way through. Only Stanley Matthews was spared the blushes, rested by Winterbottom.

H
Highest attendance ever for a World Cup finals game was between Uruguay and Brazil at the Maracanã stadium, 199,854 fans crowded this famous arena.

I
India qualified for the World Cup but withdrew because FIFA wouldn't let them play in bare feet!

J
The World Cup was renamed the **Jules** Rimet Trophy to celebrate the 25th anniversary of Rimet's presidency of FIFA.

K
Knock-out was ahem...knocked out, in favour of going back to a group format. Some routes easier than others. Four groups: 4 in 2 groups, 3 in another, and 2 in the last. Winners would contest a final group, and the winners would win the World Cup.

L
Chilean **linesman** Sergio Bustamante was the youngest official in any finals match: 26 years 65 days in the group game between Brazil and Switzerland.

M
Stan **Mortenson** of Blackpool has the ultimate accolade of scoring England's' first ever WORLD CUP goal on the 24th June in Rio de Janeiro v Chile.

N
Not one 0-0 score line in the tournament, and not even one in the history of the finals to date. Even though the Brazilians would have taken a draw for the final match.

O
Olympic champions of 1948 Sweden were coached by George Rayner of England, and made it to the final group, but were put to the sword emphatically by Brazil 7-1. They lost the best of their players to the Italian league, the Swedish FA refused to pick them to go to the World Cup. They were the first team to beat a World Cup winning team beating Italy 3-2.

P
A **plane** crashes a year before the finals wiped out Torino's quadruple league champions, thus decimating the Italian team of eight of its best players, but shaming other teams who withdrew, they came to compete, even if only for two matches. Unluckily they came second and failed to qualify for the final group. The Italian team sailed to Brazil. The team hardly surprisingly refused to fly.

Q
Qualification was a farce yet again. Scotland refused to enter, because they wanted to go as British champions, but came second in their Home Nations group. Argentina wouldn't go because of their fierce rivalry with the hosts. Others qualified but withdrew. 13 teams made the journey in the end, out of 32.

R
George **Reader** of England is the oldest ref to take control of a game at a World Cup at the age of 56 years and 236 days, and the first Englishman to officiate a World Cup finals final match (as such. Uruguay v Brazil)

S
The Maracanã **Stadium** was built for the finals but was still unfinished when the tournament began, but still hosted the opening game. 5000 pigeons and a 21-gun salute opened the new arena, which

it didn't take to. Arthur Ellis, and others in the stands were peppered with a shower of concrete, fortunately none were big blocks. Twice the capacity of Wembley, it holds the record for the top 4 largest attendances in World Cup history.

T
Top scorer of the WORLD CUP was Ademir of Brazil with 8 goals, 4 of which came against Sweden. The blue eyed, pencil moustache, Jimmy Hill chinned forward alongside Jair and Zizinho was a force to be reckoned with. Sources say if TV had been there we would be talking about the supreme skills and talents of Ademir, not Pelé.

U
Uruguay became the winners again. Two tournaments entered, two won...not bad. Against the odds they had to beat the formidable Brazil in the final group game to become champions, they did 2-1, after being a goal down. The term 'Maracanazo' was coined, which roughly translates as 'The Maracanã Blow'.

V
Vast travelling was on the cards for everyone but Brazil, who played their group, games in the then capital Rio de Janeiro. The rest had to travel thousands of miles from one corner to another in this massive country.

W
WW2 interrupted the World Cup for 20 years, and this was the first peacetime finals. Germany was still in exile, and other countries were still reeling from the war, so didn't enter.

X
Final XI from final group game: Uruguay: Maspoli, M Gonzalez, Tejera, Gambetta, Varela ©, Rodriguez, Andrade, **Ghiggia (79)**, Perez, Miguez, **Schiaffino (66)**, Ruben Moran
Brazil: Barbosa, Augusto ©, Juvenal, Bauer, Danilo, Bigode, **Friaca (47),** Zizinho, Ademir, Jair, Chico

Y

Yugoslavia had a team that was master passes. In 2 games they rattled in 7 goals. They started the match v Brazil with 10 men, Mitic cut his head on an exposed girder in the changing rooms of the unfinished Maracanã, and came on when they were 1-0 down, eventually losing 2-0. They won the first ever finals game to be played under floodlights 3-0 v Switzerland.

Z

Telmo **Zarraonanadia** 'Zarra' was probably the first of the great Spanish forwards to grace the big stage. He scored 4 goals in 6 games and scored the winner v England to send them home.

WORLD CUP 1954

WEST GERMANY V HUNGARY
3-2

FIFA World Cup A-Z of Facts and Figures

TEAM	STANDING	P	W	D	L	F-A
WEST GERMANY	CHAMPS	6*	5	0	1	25-14
HUNGARY	RU	5	4	0	1	27-10
AUSTRIA	SF	5	4	0	1	17-12
URUGUAY	SF	5	3	0	2	16-9
BRAZIL	QF	3	1	1	1	8-5
ENGLAND	QF	3	1	1	1	8-8
YUGOSLAVIA	QF	3	1	1	1	2-3
SWITZERLAND	QF	4*	2	0	2	11-11
TURKEY	R1	3*	1	0	2	10-11
ITALY	R1	3*	1	0	2	6-7
FRANCE	R1	2	1	0	1	3-3
BELGIUM	R1	2	0	1	1	5-8
MEXICO	R1	2	0	0	2	2-8
CZECHOSLOVAKIA	R1	2	0	0	2	0-7
SCOTLAND	R1	2	0	0	2	0-8
SOUTH KOREA	R1	2	0	0	2	0-16

*Swiss last Quarter Finalist via playoff
*Best record after playoff loss

FIFA World Cup A-Z of Facts and Figures

A
Austria was still a team to be reckoned with but was growing old. Their amazing comeback v Switzerland (3-0 down) and thrashing of the Czech's (5-0), held them in good stead. They got battered though v W Germany in the semi's 6-1, with the Walter bros, Franz and Ottmar scoring 4. They beat Uruguay 3-1 for 3rd place.

B
Berne's Wankdorf stadium was the setting for what was the biggest shock in WORLD CUP history for a final. With Puskas half fit after his injury in their previous encounter, Hungary were half the team they could be. Still they went two up in nine minutes, Puskas scoring the first. W Germany came back and was incredibly level after 19 minutes. The winner came with 5 minutes remaining from Rahn, and the juggernaut was stopped.

C'
Clockwork' a nickname given to the dynamo Ernst Ocwirk by the English, because of his penalty box to penalty box runs. The last great attacking centre half, was Austria's captain, and best player by far. Fittingly scored the last goal in the 3rd place game, in the World Cup's 100th finals game.

D
Team was **drawn** out of a hat which was the way the Quarter finals were decided for the knock-out stage. Group winners could play each other in this round, and the semis. When will FIFA learn?

E
England got through there group as winners, but at the expense of Stan Matthews injured with a bruised toe but was fit to play Uruguay. England lost 4-2, and the blame was put directly at keeper Merrick, who was to blame for 3 goals. He never played for his country again. England played well, but with an average age of 30, the players tired, and couldn't get back in the game.

FIFA World Cup A-Z of Facts and Figures

F

First World Cup to be televised, and probably Hungary v Brazil was the first video nasty. Arthur Ellis was the ref, who had to send off someone for the first time for him in an international. In fact, he sent off 3 players. There were stampings, players chasing each other, and fisticuffs galore. A free-for-all broke out as the teams left the pitch, with photographers attacking police, and Puskas supposedly splitting Pinheiro's head open, so Brazil retaliated by throwing glass into the Hungarian's changing room, after the lights went unexpectedly out. Hungary won 'The Battle of Berne' 4-2.

G

Groups for this WORLD CUP were slightly different than before, FIFA cannot help but tinker. In each group there were 2 seeded teams, who would only play the non-seeded teams. Any games level after 90 minutes and extra-time and the result would stand. Confusing!!

H

Hungary was the first real strong favourites going into any World Cup, unbeaten in 28 games, since 1950, and Olympic champs. Top scorers in the finals with 27(a record), and an average per game of 5.4(a finals record), goal difference of +17. Also recorded the joint biggest winning margin in WORLD CUP history 9-0 v Korea Rep. In their last warm up game before the World Cup they beat England 7-1. A juggernaut of a team.

I

Injections of Vitamin C at half-time were presumed to have been given to the German team to boost their stamina, by a Soviet sports doctor's needle. This is strongly denied by the teammates but does explain the jaundice looking players following the World Cup win.

J St **Jakob** stadium in Basle saw W Germany v Hungary, score 3-8. Who would have thought after this that Germany would win the trophy? Herberger the German manager sent out a weakened team, learning how good Hungary was. Liebrich nobbled Puskas, who had to withdraw from this game, and the next 2. Liebrich was specially picked for this game, probably to nullify Puskas. It succeeded.

K
Sandor **Kocsis** was top scorer for the WORLD CUP with 11 goals in 5 games and scored 2 or more goals in 4 consecutive games; still a record, and the first player to score 2 hat-tricks at a World Cup (consecutively). A legend at heading the ball, he had a neck so thick it looked deformed. 75 goals in 68 games. Awesome!!

L
Largest goal difference improvement in consecutive games goes to Turkey and West Germany. Turkey lost 1-4 vs Germany, and then beat South Korea 7-0. W Germany lost 3-8 v Hungary (first team to lose a match and win World Cup), and winning Turkey 7-2. Turkey also have the unwanted distinction of the worst scoreline turnaround in successive games; 7-0 v Korea, and 2-7 v W Germany.

M
Most goals scored in one game Austria v Switzerland 7-5, 5-4 at half time, and Austria were 0-3 down, never had a team come back from such a deficit. Also, in this World Cup of goals came the highest scoring draw 4-4aet England v Belgium. Poor old Hong Duk-Yung of Korea as let in the most goals at a final's tournament; 16.

N
Nineteen 54, saw the 50th anniversary of FIFA, and where a better place to hold the tournament than in its own backyard. Switzerland was chosen to be the hosts in 1946.

O
Olympics in 1952 saw Hungary beat South Korea 12-0, with poor Hong Duk-Yung of Korea in goal. In the 9-0 game, midfielder Chung Nam-Sik sat down exhausted, and Buzanszky gave him a leg massage.

P
Ferenc **Puskas** and Kocsis scored 158 international goals between them. Puskas was the star of the team, and incomparable in his day. The Galloping Major (referring to his army rank,) was the most talented and inspirational leader, and knitted the team together. Half fit he nearly dragged his team to the trophy, with a disallowed goal given offside by the Welsh authoritarian official Mervyn Griffiths. 85 games, 84 goals say it all.

Q
Qualifying consisted of 38 entries where 16 went to the finals. The Saar (state of Germany) entered, Turkey got to the finals on the toss of a coin v Spain after a playoff. Poland withdrew to send Hungary there.

R
Referees with the most amazing occupational names were Charlie Faultless (Scotland), and Paul Wyssling (Swiss.) Would have been great if there were an Arthur Side as linesman (Offside???)

S
Scotland made the trip to Switzerland for their first finals. Managed by their first national manager Andy Beattie they faced Austria; lost 1-0 and Beattie resigned. So, they played their next, and last game v holders Uruguay, and ruefully lost 7-0. Tommy Docherty the Scot defender says that Willie Cunningham captain and fullback got a 'sunburned tongue' trying to contain the irrepressible Schiaffino.

T
The German **team** became the only one to win the World Cup with amateur players (German league was not professional until season 1963-4), and probably ever will likely be the only team ever. Whilst the Hungarians were *de jure* amateurs like in all communist countries at that time, and all were playing professional football.

U
Uruguay finally lost a finals game after 24 years. They lost in the semis to Hungary, in one of the all-time great games. Both teams

were not at full strength, Hungary were rampant and were 2 up, but the Uruguayans were battlers, and were level with 3 minutes to go. Extra time was a bridge to far though, and Hungary ran away 4-2 winners. End to end for 120 minutes of elegant football heaven.

V
Venues for the finals were this time in proximity of Berne. With 6 cities picked to hold the games.

W
West Germany won their first World Cup, and go down as the highest goal scorers for WORLD CUP winners; 25, but also most goals conceded; 14. The first finals team apparently to wear screw in studs, which some say helped in their final win v Hungary.

X
Final XI: West Germany: Turek, Posipal, Kohlmeyer, Eckel, Liebrich, Mai, **Rahn (19,85)**, **Morlock (10)**, Walter O, Walter F(c), Schafer

Hungary: Grosics, Buzanszky, Lantos, Bozsik, Lorant, Zakarias, **Czibor (8)**, Kocsis, Hidegkuti, **Puskas (c)(6)**, Toth J

Y
Youngest captain of a World Cup team in the finals was Turgay Seren of Turkey he was 22 years 33 days. Ladislav Novak of Czechoslovakia was 22 years 193 days.

Z
Zero-Zero still a score that still eludes this amazing competition, and let's face it, in a tournament that was exploding with goals, it was never going to happen. Austria v Scotland 1-0 was the closest score.

WORLD CUP 1958

BRAZIL V SWEDEN
5-2

FIFA World Cup A-Z of Facts and Figures

TEAM	STANDING	P	W	D	L	F-A
BRAZIL	CHAMPS	6	5	1	0	16-4
SWEDEN	RU	6	4	1	1	12-7
FRANCE	SF	6	4	0	2	23-15
WEST GERMANY	SF	6	2	2	2	12-14
YUGOSLAVIA	QF	4	1	2	1	7-7
WALES	QF	5*	1	3	1	4-4
SOVIET UNION	QF	5*	2	1	2	5-6
N IRELAND	QF	5*	2	1	2	6-10
CZECHOSLOVAKIA	R1	4*	1	1	2	9-6
HUNGARY	R1	4*	1	1	2	7-5
ENGLAND	R1	4*	0	3	1	4-5
PARAGUAY	R1	3	1	1	1	9-12
ARGENTINA	R1	3	1	0	2	5-10
SCOTLAND	R1	3	0	1	2	4-6
AUSTRIA	R1	3	0	1	2	2-7
MEXICO	R1	3	0	1	2	1-8

*Playoffs to get out of the group stage.

FIFA World Cup A-Z of Facts and Figures

A
Argentina entered the fold again, having won the Copa America in '57, and scoring 25 goals in 6 matches were one of the favourites to win, but finished bottom of their group, needing only a draw in their last game to qualify lost 6-1 to Czechoslovakia. Stabile's reign as manager came to an end after 17 years at the helm.

B
Brazil won their first World Cup. Now an athletic and artistic team, who played with more flair, the final had the most goals scored by one team; Brazil, and by both teams 7; Sweden scoring 2, in any final in World Cup history. They became the first country to win the WORLD CUP outside its own continent. Sweden's fans applauded Brazil on their lap of honour because of the manner which they won the WORLD CUP.

C
The **colours** of the Brazilian kit were the ones that we are used to seeing today. The yellow shirts and blue shorts were first used this year, but for the final Sweden played in Yellow, Brazil had not bought an away kit, so had to hastily find some blue shirts and sow their badge from the yellow shirts onto them and play.

D
A **dentist** and psychologist travelled with the Brazilian team. A dentist because a lot of the players had dental problems, due to the poor hygiene in the townships back in Brazil, thus causing infections. A psychologist because some of the players were still traumatized by the 1950 World Cup defeat v Uruguay.

E
England drew their 3 group games and lost the play-off game v USSR 1-0. A young Bobby Charlton, who had scored 3 in 2 games before the finals, never played a game. Billy Wright was captain for his 3rd finals, a joint record.

F
Coach **Feola** of Brazil was very shrewd, and seeing that Sweden used wingers very well, dropped de Sordi, and in came Djalma for his 1st game of the WORLD CUP. Ruthless and right. He also was said to take naps in training and would sometimes close his eyes when watching a game giving the impression that he was asleep. Some say Didi was the real coach because he commanded the midfield.

G
Garrincha the twisted-legged winger from birth made his debut with Pelé in their second game v USSR and hit the bar in the first minute (Pelé in the 2nd.) A mesmerizing player ran the Swedes ragged in the final, setting up the 1st two goals, swaying the game Brazil's way.

H
Hungary were hindered by the 1956 revolution, crushed by Moscow, and had no Puskas, Kocsis or Czibor, whilst the others were past their best. They were beat by Wales in a play-off for the Quarterfinals 2-1, in an eerily sounding stadium, due to that the day before the leader of the Hungarian uprising had been executed. Banners draped in black and Free Hungarian chanting entailed.

I
Italy again really sent a reserve side for qualifying for the finals, leaving their front 3 of Sivori-Maschio-Angelillo at home. They again picked from South America, in this case Schiaffino and Ghiggia. They failed to qualify losing out to N Ireland, the first and only time Italy has failed to make it.

J
Just Fontaine of France holds the record as the Top scorer in World Cup finals history with 13 goals in one tournament. He scored in each match he played in, and scored in 6 consecutive games, and scored 2 in 4 consecutive games. Jointly record holder with most hatricks in World Cup's with 2. France top scored the finals with 23 goals, just was second choice behind Rene Bliard, but he got injured, and the rest is history.

K
Heinz **Kwiatkowski** the German keeper let in 4 goals for the second tournament running to be the tournaments leading scorers. These two games were his only matches in the finals.

L
Nils **Liedholm** of Sweden is the oldest goal scorer in a World Cup final to date, aged 35 years 263 days. Sweden recalled Englishman George Raynor as coach, and this time picked players who played in Italy, justifying that with their best players they could go all the way......nearly. Maybe their new vey short-back-and-sides for the final sapped their strength.

M
Mazzola (Jose Altafini) the Brazilian striker scored 2 in their opening game, but his last game was v Wales. He and Pelé were the future of Brazil, an average age of 18, but Vava took his place. Named after his resemblance to Valentino Mazzola who died in the Turin team's air crash of 1949. Jose later played for Italy.

N
N Ireland reached the Quarters via the play-offs beating the Czech's 2-1. They were beaten convincingly by France 4-0, a game to far for the walking wounded. Gregg the keeper who got injured earlier in the WORLD CUP had to play, even though he was using a walking stick to get around with in their hotel.

O
Olympic champions USSR entered for the first time, with the legendry Yashin in goal, and reached the Quarters before being knocked out by Sweden 2-0. A regimental team, of fantastic fitness, they were one of the favourites pre-World Cup.

P
Pelé is the youngest player ever to score in a WORLD CUP final, he was 17 years 249 days old, and he scored two. He is also the youngest player to score a hat-trick at the finals v France 5 days earlier, and the

youngest player to score in World Cup history v Wales aged 17 years 239 days.

Q
Qualifying consisted of 53 entries, with 16 going to the finals. No Home Nation games. Africa/Asia through up the usual cock up, with withdrawals. Indonesia won, then withdrew, Sudan got a walkover, because Egypt withdrew, then they withdrew. Ended up Israel had no-one to play, so ended up playing best 2nd placed team, Wales and lost. Glad that's clear.

R
Helmut **Rahn** of West Germany carried on where he left of in the '54 World Cup and scored 2 goals in the 1st game of '58. Only playing after Herberger, the manager told him to 'reduce his lager intake or don't play.' He scored 6 goals in all, helping Germany to 4th place.

S
Scotland's Bobby Collins scored the 500th World Cup goal v Yugoslavia. They finished bottom of their group with 1 point.

T
The **tournaments** format on this occasion, unlike 1954, the group rivals would all play each other. The groups had at least 1 West European team, 1 East European team, 1 of the British teams, and 1 from the American continent. If the points were the same after all games played, then a play-off would be contested to determine who would progress.

U
The **UK** for the first and only time had all nations present, but the Munich plane crash earlier that year affected 3 of them, plus part-time Scotland manager Matt Busby.

V
A record 12 **venues** for the finals were used. The final being played in Stockholm's Rasunda Stadium.

W
Wales were eliminated in qualifying by the Czech's, but got an 11th hour reprieve, when Israel was not allowed to go without playing a game. So, Wales were pulled out of the hat, and beat Israel 2-0 in both legs. They reached their best finals place in the Quarters, finally beaten by Brazil 1-0.

X
Final XI: Brazil: Gylmar, Djalma Santos, N Santos, Zito, Bellini(c), Orlando, Garrincha, Didi, **Vava (9,32), Pelé (55,90), Zagallo (68)**
    Sweden: Svensson, Bergmark, Axbom, Borjesson, Gustavsson, Parling, Hamrin, Gren, **Simonsson (80), Liedholm(c)(4),** Skoglund

Y
Youngest referee ever to officiate a game was Juan Gardeazabal from Spain. He was 24 years 193 days old; he refereed France v Paraguay 7-3.

Z
The first **Zero-Zero** in WORLD CUP history was the group game between England and Brazil, and the first time Brazil had failed to score in a World Cup game. England ended up drawing their 3 group games.

FIFA World Cup A-Z of Facts and Figures

WORLD CUP 1962

BRAZIL V CZECHOSLOVAKIA
3-1

FIFA World Cup A-Z of Facts and Figures

TEAM	STANDING	P	W	D	L	F-A
BRAZIL	CHAMPS	6	5	1	0	14-5
CZECHOSLOVAKIA	RU	6	3	1	2	7-7
CHILE	SF	6	4	0	2	10-8
YUGOSLAVIA	SF	6	3	0	3	10-7
HUNGARY	QF	4	2	1	1	8-3
SOVIET UNION	QF	4	2	1	1	9-7
WEST GERMANY	QF	4	2	1	1	4-2
ENGLAND	QF	4	1	1	2	5-6
ITALY	R1	3	1	1	1	3-2
ARGENTINA	R1	3	1	1	1	2-3
MEXICO	R1	3	1	0	2	3-4
SPAIN	R1	3	1	0	2	2-3
URUGUAY	R1	3	1	0	2	4-6
COLOMBIA	R1	3	1	0	2	5-11
BULGARIA	R1	3	0	1	2	1-7
SWITZERLAND	R1	3	0	0	3	2-8

FIFA World Cup A-Z of Facts and Figures

A
Aymore Moreira Brazil's coach, drafted in pre-World Cup when Feola fell ill, was the brother of Zeze Moreira, who was Brazil's manager in 1954, becoming the only brothers to coach teams in the finals.

B
Battle of Santiago between Chile and Italy as gone down in folklore as one of the dirtiest games ever. From the start the Chileans allegedly spat in the Italians faces. Ref Aston (Eng) sent off Ferrini for retaliation, which upheld the game for 8 minutes. Punches were thrown, David was sent off for kicking Sanchez in the neck. The Italians were later stoned at their training camp. Oh and, Chile won 2-0.

C
Czechoslovakia's' Vaclav Masek has the honour of scoring the World Cups' fastest ever goal, to date v Mexico, timed at 15 seconds, but in the end, Mexico won 3-1.

D
Carlos **Dittborn** president of Chile's FA argued that Chile deserved to host the World Cup because in his words 'We have nothing.' He died just before the finals started at the age of 38, the stadium Arica was named after him. Two years earlier an earthquake damaged two-thirds of the buildings beyond repair, and with only one stadium of World Cup credentials odds were stacked against him, but he prevailed through sheer determination.

E
England again started slowly, losing to Hungary, and then beating Argentina. Finally, a bore draw v Bulgaria, which Bobby Moore said was 'One of the worst internationals of all time'. In the Quarters they met their match v Brazil and was put to the sword by a solo performance by Garrincha, losing 3-1. Bad day continued for Greaves who captured a stray dog on the pitch, only for it to pee on him. Garrincha thought this hilarious, and after the game took the dog home to be his pet.

FIFA World Cup A-Z of Facts and Figures

F
Foreigners were added to Spain and Italy's squads for instant success. Spain had Martinez from Paraguay, Santamaria (Uru), and the great Puskas (Hun), and an injured Di Stefano (who never played a single World Cup final game). Italy had Miscio and Sivori (Arg), and Altafini, Sormani from Brazil.

G
Goal average (later goal difference) would now sensibly be used in the group stages for teams that finished level on points. The day of the play-offs was officially over.

H
Hosts Chile was not expected to qualify from there group of Germanys, Italy and the Swiss, but did, and went all the way to the semi-finals, eventually losing to Brazil. They won the third-place play-off and ended their tournament with their heads held high managed by the astute Riera.

I
Incredibly there were no less than 6 top scorers. The list is: Albert (Hun), Ivanov (USSR), Garrincha (Bra), Sanchez (Chil), Jerkovic (Yug), and Vava (Bra), all scoring 4 goals.

J
Two Italian **journalists** reported the poverty and nocturnal activities of the women of Chile then fled the country, leaving the national team to bear the brunt of the Chileans. Resulting in the notorious Battle of Santiago.

K
Kucero Czechoslovakia's regular recognized striker was missing from the finals, so for them to reach the final was a feat to be recognized. They played superbly; drawing v Brazil in the group games, then convincingly beat Hungary and Yugoslavia in the knock-out stages. One nil up in the final, but against lesser opposition they could have been champions.

FIFA World Cup A-Z of Facts and Figures

L
Juan Carlos **Lorenzo** Argentina's new coach, and later one of the all-time great managers, was now in charge. A bullish, take no prisoners coach, instilling this into his team. He would identify the opposition's best players and stopped them playing...by any means. Against Bulgaria 2 players were injured and ended their World Cup. Thankfully they didn't qualify for the next stage. Lorenzo would later manage a Lazio team that attacked Arsenal in a street, have 3 sent off v Celtic, and Boca. Argentina's coach in 1978 refused to pick any players from Lorenzo's Boca squad.

M
Mexico at the 14th attempt and on their captains 33rd birthday won their first finals match v Czechoslovakia 3-1.

N
1962 was the last WORLD CUP which could not be televised live in Europe because it just predated the arrival of satellite and the start of live transmissions from America to Europe. In the United Kingdom, the BBC broadcast live radio commentaries and film recordings of matches on television two days late.

O
The only WORLD CUP **Olympic** goal (straight from a corner) was scored during the finals by Colombia's Coll v USSR in the incredible 4-4 draw. Columbia was 3-0 down after 13 minutes but managed to pull of the greatest WORLD CUP comeback, and nearly won it in the dying minutes.

P
Pelé only played in the first 2 games, scored 1 goal, but got a groin injury v Czechoslovakia, and his WORLD CUP was over. Still picked up a 2nd winners medal though, at the age of 21. His replacement Amarildo scored 2 in his first game v Spain.

Q
Qualifying had 56 entrants that whittled down to 16 teams in the finals. No African or Asian teams made it, each playing sub-groups

from the same continent, then playing a final match v a European opposition, and losing. Italy qualified playing only 2 games v Israel, the least amount of games to qualify for these Championships.

R
The communist **regime** of Hungary denied them of the services of Kocsis, Czibor and Puskas, who all lived in exile from their homeland. Although a new hot prospect was on the horizon, whose name was Florin Albert. An exceptional forward, who scored a hat-trick v Bulgaria, and the winner v England. Hungary's' luck ran out in the Quarters v the Czech's.

S
Semi-Final Brazil v Chile was won again by a great display from Garrincha, who terrorized the Chilean defence, scoring two. Later he was sent off after a missile was thrown from the crowd, and cutting his head, and after persistent fouling he retaliated. After strenuous backroom negotiations from Brazil, he could play in the final.

T
Title of WORLD CUP winners again would befall Brazil, and they became the 2nd team to win back to back WORLD CUP's, the last team at present to achieve this feat. 9 of their '58 squad played in '62, and the samba kings skill saw them dispose of all they met.

U
Unlucky fans who was to watch the semi-final in Vina del Mar; Brazil v Chile, instead got to watch Czechoslovakia v Yugoslavia, as the venues got switched to accommodate the Chilean team. Only 5,890 turned up to watch the 'Slavic teams, whereas 76,594 watched the South Americans. The final in the Estadio Nacional de Chile hosted 68,679 fans.

V
Vava of Brazil became the first player to score in two finals. Two goals in '58 final, and one in this WORLD CUP. Still a joint record for most goals scored by one player in the final.

W
West German coach Sepp Herberger ended his love affair with the WORLD CUP after their Quarter-Final defeat v Yugoslavia (the 3rd WORLD CUP in a row, they met). It started before the 1938 finals.

X
Final **XI: Brazil**: Gylmar, D Santos, N Santos, **Zito (69)**, Mauro (c), Zozimo, Garrincha, Didi, **Vava (78)**, **Amarildo (16)**, Zagello
Czechoslovakia: Schroif, Jiri, Tichy, Novak (c), Pluskal, Popluhar, **Masopust (14),** Pospichal, Scherer, Kadraba, Kvasnak, Jelinek

Y
Yugoslavia were the current Olympic champions and had most of their players from the fine Partizan Belgrade team. They were orchestrated through their playmaker Sekularc, and goal poacher Jerkovic. Losing out in the semis to the Czech's was disappointing, but beating the Germans, after so many defeats was heartwarming.

Z
Zagallo, Zito et al, warmed to the Chilean crowd after winning the semi-final, by parading the Chilean flag around the stadium on a lap of honour. Throughout the WORLD CUP Zagallos' lung power, and skills transformed Brazil from 4-4-2 to an attacking 4-3-3. Zito's goal in the final was the nail in the coffin of the Czech comeback.

WORLD CUP 1966

ENGLAND V WEST GERMANY
4-2 aet

FIFA World Cup A-Z of Facts and Figures

TEAM	STANDING	P	W	D	L	F-A
ENGLAND	CHAMPS	6	5	1	0	11-3
WEST GERMANY	RU	6	4	1	1	15-6
PORTUGAL	SF	6	5	0	1	17-8
SOVIET UNION	SF	6	4	0	2	10-6
ARGENTINA	QF	4	2	1	1	4-2
HUNGARY	QF	4	2	0	2	8-7
URUGUAY	QF	4	1	2	1	2-5
NORTH KOREA	QF	4	1	1	2	5-9
ITALY	R1	3	1	0	2	2-2
SPAIN	R1	3	1	0	2	4-5
BRAZIL	R1	3	1	0	2	4-6
MEXICO	R1	3	0	2	1	1-3
CHILE	R1	3	0	1	2	2-5
FRANCE	R1	3	0	1	2	2-5
BULGARIA	R1	3	0	0	3	1-8
SWITZERLAND	R1	3	0	0	3	1-9

FIFA World Cup A-Z of Facts and Figures

A
Albrecht of the dirty Argentines was the first player to be sent off in the finals for kneeing Weber of W Germany in the groin, which must have been a formidable part of his anatomy; Albrecht left the field limping. The game finished 0-0.

B
Brazil scored the first goal of the tournament through Pelé's 13th minute thunderous free kick v Bulgaria. Brazil had now gone 13 games unbeaten in WORLD CUP's (1958-66.) Bulgaria's coach Vytlacils' last WORLD CUP coaching game was also v Brazil; the 1962 WORLD CUP final.

C
Antonio **Carbajal** aged 37 played his final game in goal for Mexico in his 5th finals, and kept a clean sheet drawing 0-0 with Uruguay at Wembley. Carbajal's WORLD CUP playing career spanned a world record 16 years and 25 days (1950-66.)

D
Gotfried **Dienst** the Swiss ref eventually awarded Hurst's goal, and thus making him the first and only to date to score a hat-trick (and ultimate;1 with head and both feet. Hurst also first to score with his head) in a WORLD CUP final. Dienst also is only 1 of 2 referees to officiate a WORLD CUP final and a European Championships final in 1968. Both controversial.

E
England win their first and to date only WORLD CUP. Omens were on England's side in the final; the infamous Hurst goal, and every team who scored first in the final since the war, had gone on to lose the game. England won the trophy scoring the least amount of goals and least amount of goals conceded F11 A3.

F
Fuhrer and Eichmann of Switzerland played in W Germanys group. They sound familiar.

FIFA World Cup A-Z of Facts and Figures

G
Garrincha played his 50th a last game for his country v Hungary. This was the great man's only ever defeat in the colours of his nation, an amazing fete.

H
Hungary's Bene scored in all their finals games and played a part in all the other goals. Still played for them in 1979. Once scored all 6 goals in a 6-0-win v Morocco in the 1964 Olympics. Not bad for a winger!!

I
Injuries to Pelé v Bulgaria stopped his participation in Brazil's second game. He was still injured going into the final must win game v Portugal and came out of the game nearly paralyzed by the rough malicious knee-high tackling which went unpunished by English ref McCabe. Pelé had to be carried off.

J
Jack Charlton in the semi's deliberately handballed Torres' header, and gave away a penalty which Eusebio converted. If that happened today Jack would have missed the final, but for refereeing favouritism from a European official.

K
N **Korea** represented Asia and its 2 billion people, along with USSR. Not one of the Koreans stood higher than 5'8", including their keeper Lee Chan-myung; who at 19 was the youngest in any finals tournament. They also pulled off one of the biggest WORLD CUP shocks ever when they beat Italy 1-0, thanks to Park Doo-ik's goal, he later became a dentist. The Italians went home to a barrage of tomatoes and other missiles. Korea went on to narrowly lose 5-3 to Portugal having gone 3-0 up.

L
A **lion** symbolizing England, named World Cup Willie became the first WORLD CUP mascot. He wore a Union Jack Flag jersey with 'World Cup' emblazed on it.

M
Mozambique was the birthplace of Eusebio the WORLD CUP top scorer. First and only time an Africa born player has done this. 4 of his 9 goals were from the penalty spot and scored 4 against N Korea.

N
No home countries. N Ireland missed out on play-off by drawing to Albania. Wales lost to Greece. Scotland lost to Italy with a much-depleted team due to injuries and club bosses depriving them of their world class players. Jock Stein resigned as manager.

O
Opening game of the WORLD CUP England v Uruguay was delayed because 7 of the England players left their identity cards at their hotel. A dispatch motorcyclist had to fetch them. Also, this was the first WORLD CUP to have drug testing.

P
Portugal's' first finals topping their qualifying group that contained the 1962 runners up Czechoslovakia, thus knocking them out. Eusebio scoring the only goal in Bratislava. They eventually lost to Bobby Charlton's 2 goals in the semi. After Bobby's second goal Augusto shook his hand; remarkable.

Q
Qualifying consisted of 71 teams, and again there were funny stories. All the African nations withdrew after FIFA refuse to guarantee them their own qualifying pool, as did most of Asia. S Korea withdrew leaving N Korea to beat Australia in Cambodia to qualify. After Syria withdrew it left Spain and Eire to play each other for a place in the finals. They each won their home games; Eire 1-0, Spain 4-1, and after a play off in Paris the Spanish went through. This was before the days of goal difference, otherwise Belgium who topped their group on goal difference would have qualified, not Bulgaria.

R
Stanley **Rous** the president of FIFA had allegedly told referees to go easy on the European virile style of play. This accumulated in the

more gifted players getting hacked out of the tournament, as well as S American players getting sent off against European teams. Argentina was an exception to the rule; brutal and cunning with their atrocious fouling and spitting deserved to be dumped out of the WORLD CUP.

S
Stampex exhibition in Westminster is where the WORLD CUP trophy was stolen from; a week later it was found by Pickles the dog in a hedge in SE London.

T
Total and unmitigated disaster' the words of Pelé to sum up brazils WORLD CUP effort. Relying on veterans from previous WORLD CUP's, and new blood that was a WORLD CUP to early.

U
Uruguay's Ondino Viera was the first example of a coach to pick his son (Milton) to play in WORLD CUP finals. They got knocked out in the quarters by W Germany 4-0, after a vicious game with fouls galore by both teams. With the ref siding with the Germans, the Uruguayans had a man sent off for a stomach high tackle, then slapping Seelers face on his way off. A police escort was deemed appropriate.

V
Venues for the finals consisted of 8 stadiums; Wembley, White City, Goodison, Old Trafford, Hillsborough, Villa Park, Roker Park and Ayresome Park. England's semi v Portugal should have been played at Goodison, but officials changed it at the last minute to Wembley fearing a loss to debutants Portugal. White City a stadium made for the 1908 Olympics was used for 1 match between Uruguay and France because greyhound racing was on at Wembley.

W
Wingers that were used by England in the WORLD CUP Paine and Connelly were never capped again. Callaghan didn't play again until 1977, a gap of 11 years 59 days, still the England record. Group games for England were all played with wingers. The wingless

wonders team came from the quarter finals onwards. Also, England's goals v Mexico (2-0) and France (2-0) in their group games were all scored in the 36th and 76th minutes.

X
Final XI England: Banks, Cohen, Wilson, Stiles, Charlton J, Moore (c), Ball, Hunt, Charlton B, **Hurst (18,101,120), Peters (78)**

W Germany: Tilkowski, Hottges, Schnellinger, Beckenbauer, Schulz, **Weber (89),** Held, **Haller (12),** Seeler (c), Overath, Emmerich

Y
Only 30 odd **years** later did Geoff Hurst get the match ball for his hat-trick, because in Germany the player who scores the first goal of the game gets the ball, this being Helmut Haller.

Z
Zsolt of Hungary was the referee who had the privilege to officiate the opening game of the finals a 0-0 draw between England and Uruguay.

WORLD CUP 1970

BRAZIL V ITALY
4-1

FIFA World Cup A-Z of Facts and Figures

TEAM	STANDING	P	W	D	L	F-A
BRAZIL	CHAMPS	6	6	0	0	19-7
ITALY	RU	6	3	2	1	10-8
WEST GERMANY	SF	6	5	0	1	17-10
URUGUAY	SF	6	2	1	3	4-5
SOVIET UNION	QF	4	2	1	1	6-2
MEXICO	QF	4	2	1	1	6-4
PERU	QF	4	2	1	1	9-9
ENGLAND	QF	4	2	0	2	4-4
SWEDEN	R1	3	1	1	1	2-2
BELGIUM	R1	3	1	0	2	4-5
ROMANIA	R1	3	1	0	2	4-5
ISRAEL	R1	3	0	2	1	1-3
BULGARIA	R1	3	0	1	2	5-9
MOROCCO	R1	3	0	1	2	2-6
CZECHOSLOVAKIA	R1	3	0	0	3	2-7
EL SALVADOR	R1	3	0	0	3	0-9

FIFA World Cup A-Z of Facts and Figures

A
Victor Esparrago of Uruguay has a surname in English that means **asparagus**. Victor is also known in his local town as 'The man with smelly wee.'

B
Juan Ignacio **Basaguren** of Mexico became the first substitute to score in a WORLD CUP tournament, scoring against El Salvador.

C
Morocco's had a French coach in qualifying with the comical name of **Clouseau**, but they were no laughing matter during the finals, when they became the first African team to avoid defeat in the game v Bulgaria (1-1).

D
Referee **De Moraes** of Brazil was rumoured to have asked for money to 'sway' the match Sweden's way v Uruguay. FIFA switched him to referee Italy v Israel to diffuse the already growing tensions that existed about 'dubious official decisions in this WORLD CUP. Sweden won 1-0 anyway.

E
El Salvador qualified after 3 games against rivals Honduras, which incited a war between the two nations (probably immigration was the factor, but football sounds better.) 3000 people lost their lives. They lost all 3 games without scoring, but controversy wasn't far away (see K).

F
The **final** in the 100,000 plus Azteca Stadium was between the defence minded Italians, against the free flowing forward thinking Brazilian's. Brazil won 4-1, with probably the greatest goal in WORLD CUP history to end a wonderful tournament, scored by captain Carlos Alberto.

G
Guanajuato, Leon was the venue when W Germany got payback for 1966. England leading 2-0 with 30 minutes to go, threw it away, or was it a glorious comeback? Or even Banks' food poisoning (Montezuma's Revenge.) Newton, Labone, B Charlton and Bonetti never played for England again.

H
Heatstroke was a major issue, playing in 100°F, the Europeans being the worst affected. Dobrin of Romania missed the tournament due to it. England used 'slow sodium' tablets to counter the heat and exhaustion.

I
Italy were European Champions and became the first team to win their group by only scoring 1 goal. They reached the final probably exhausted due to the near intolerable heat in the semi against W Germany. Antonio Juliano became the first substitute to come on in a WORLD CUP final.

J
Joao Saldhana a journalist was such a detractor of the national team, that eventually the Brazilian Federation gave into his criticism and gave him the manager's job! They cruised the qualifying, but his short fuse and fondness to settle arguments with his fists soon became his downfall. Zagallo took over for the finals.

K
Ali **Kandil** the referee for the match El Salvador v Mexico caused uproar by playing on when the Salvador team thought they had a throw in, resulting in a goal. The players responded by jostling officials and gesturing to be booked. Kandil never refereed another finals match.

L
Landmark game for some of England's players came in the match v Czechoslovakia. Bobby Charlton played his world record equalling 105th cap, and Allan Clarke had the feat of scoring on his debut, his

wife's birthday and their wedding anniversary. Jack Charlton played his last England game as did Jeff Astle.

M
Most goals scored in extra time are 5, in the great semi-final between Italy-W Germany. 1-1 at full time this ding doing game saw two exhausted teams go toe to toe, until Rivera broke German hearts with a 111th minute winner, after Muller had scored the equaliser in the 110th minute. One of the greats.

N
Thomas **Nordhal** of Sweden had an Uncle Knut who played in WORLD CUP '50, and his father Gunner, and another, Uncle Bertil both played for their country.

O
A fact those 2 years earlier in the **Olympics**, some competitors needed oxygen. FIFA decided to overlook the fact of heat and altitude problems were rife throughout the WORLD CUP and didn't consider it. In fact, they decided to play matches at noon to accommodate TV.

P
Peru qualified courtesy of Argentina, and under the manager ship of Didi a Brazilian legend. They arrived at the WORLD CUP in tragedy, after an earthquake devastated the country. A minute's silence was performed at the start of their match v Bulgaria. Cubillas was their outstanding player scoring in every match (5 goals in 4 matches).

Q
Qualifying consisted of 70 entries, and for the first time FIFA allowed Asian and African continents a qualifying competition. Big names to miss out were Argentina who only drew v Peru 2-2, and Portugal who finished bottom of their group.

R
Alf **Ramsey** England's manager bought extra pressure on his players by having a 'prickly' relationship with the press. This resulted in

Mexican fans making as much noise as they could at night outside the England camp, as well as being very hostile at every match.

S
The players to have **Scored** in most tournaments to date were Pelé and Seeler each chalking up 4 tournaments 1958-62-66-70, with at least 1 goal. Also, Jairzinho of Brazil has the accolade of being the only player to date to score in every match of a World Cup his team played in, including the final.

T
Toluca and Puebla the venues for Group 2 had the highest altitude. This maybe the reason only 6 goals were scored in the group. Toluca stadium La Bombonera, the chocolate box lies 8744ft above sea level.

U
Uruguay coach Hohberg scored 2 goals in the infamous Hungary-Uruguay match of WORLD CUP '54. Uruguay got to the semi-finals without their influential stylish playmaker captain Rocha who was injured and out of WORLD CUP in the first 13 minutes of the first game.

V
Fuego Verde (Green Fire) was the name of the jewellery shop where England's Bobby Moore got stitched up pre-WORLD CUP. The accuser Clara Padilla fled to USA, and the shop owned by Danilo Rojas got closed. Iceman Moore went on and had a near faultless WORLD CUP.

W
West Germany had an excellent WORLD CUP finishing 3rd and beating England, but only just qualified by beating Scotland 3-2 in their group game. Things could have been so different. Top **scorer** for the tournament was Gerd Muller with 10.

X
Final XI: Brazil: Félix, **Carlos Alberto(86)(c)**, Everaldo, Clodoaldo, Brito, Piazza, **Jairzinho (71), Gerson (66),** Tostao, **Pelé (18),** Rivelino

Italy: Albertosi, Burgnich, Facchetti(c), Bertini (Antonio Juliano74), Rosato, Cera, Domenghini, Mazzola, **Boninsegna (37)** (Rivera (84), De Sisti, Riva.

Y
Four **years** had passed since Pelé said he wouldn't play in another WORLD CUP; we are all glad he changed his mind. Pelé scored Brazil's first goal in the final, which was also their 100th WORLD CUP goal. Fittingly. This was also the WORLD CUP of the greatest misses of goals by Pelé (halfway shot v Czechoslovakia, and deliberate dummy around the keeper v Uruguay.) Also, he became the first player to win 3 WORLD CUP's. LEGEND.

Z
Mario **Zagallo** the star of WORLD CUP 58 and 62 took the Brazil squad to their third WORLD CUP win and became the first man to win it has a player and coach.

WORLD CUP 1974

WEST GERMANY V NETHERLANDS
2-1

FIFA World Cup A-Z of Facts and Figures

TEAM	STANDING	P	W	D	L	F-A
WEST GERMANY	CHAMPS	7	6	0	1	13-4
NETHERLANDS	RU	7	5	1	1	15-3
POLAND	SF	7	6	0	1	16-5
BRAZIL	SF	7	3	2	2	6-4
SWEDEN	R2	6	2	2	2	7-6
EAST GERMANY	R2	6	2	2	2	5-5
YUGOSLAVIA	R2	6	1	2	3	12-7
ARGENTINA	R2	6	1	2	3	9-12
SCOTLAND	R1	3	1	0	2	3-1
ITALY	R1	3	1	1	1	5-4
CHILE	R1	3	0	2	1	1-2
BULGARIA	R1	3	0	2	1	2-5
URUGUAY	R1	3	0	1	2	1-6
AUSTRALIA	R1	3	0	1	2	0-5
HAITI	R1	3	0	0	3	2-14
ZAIRE	R1	3	0	0	3	0-14

FIFA World Cup A-Z of Facts and Figures

A
Argentina needed to win final group game by 3 goals (won 4-1), and hope Italy lost (they did 2-1 v Poland to qualify from group. Then subsequently floundered bottom of group A in 2nd round.

B
Brazil was very slow starting the tournament, and only first scored in their 3rd game v Zaire. Gone had the flair and the great Pelé. They still came 3rd with their different approach of football. Ademir da Guia got his last cap in 3rd place game. His father Domingo's played for Brazil in 1938 tournament.

C
Cmokiewski of Poland came on as sub 6 times a record for a finals.

D
Denis Laws' last international game v Zaire at the age of 34, they won 2-0 at a canter, but 1 more goal would have seen them through at Brazils' expense.

E
East **Germany** beat neighbours West Germany in their only ever meeting 1-0, and caused a massive surprise, but unfortunately gave them a much tougher 2nd round group which they didn't get out of.

F
Franz Beckenbauer 'the world's first attacking sweeper' lifts the New FIFA World Cup. Rumour has it that he was orchestral in picking the team, not Schoen?

G
Gerd Muller scored the winner in the final in his last international match. Germany pre-tournament favourites had 7 of the squad play their football with the mighty Bayern Munich.

H
Holland still tinkering with their team, harnessed the nucleus of the side from the great Ajax team of the early 1970's. The term Total football was coined to remonstrate the way that Michel's team interchanged positions, and flowing football. Also, very hard players in the tackle too.

I
Image of the tournament has to be Johan Cruyffs' turn v Sweden. Cruyff was the best player in the world and used his influence by refusing to promote shirt sponsor Adidas. He had his shirt have only 2 lines down the sleeve, not their trademark 3. A truly great player, but only graced 1 World Cup.

J
Jules Rimet trophy won outright for the 3rd time by Brazil and is now theirs to keep forever…. well, it was stolen and lost for ever not long after they won it. Never to be seen again.

K
Kazadi; Zaires' keeper was replaced after only 20 minutes v Yugoslavia after conceding 3 goals. They went on to lose 9-0, a joint record. He was reinstated for the Brazil game (lost 3-0, which put Scotland out). Bwanga was his cousin who also played for Zaire.

L
Leandres brothers Fritz and Joseph – Marion of Haiti are the only brothers to come on as substitutes in a World Cup finals match (v Argentina).

M
Mwepu of Zaire was booked for charging down a free kick, and booting the ball away, before the whistle was blown v Brazil. Probably something he had seen pro's do.

N
Nicknamed 'Nose' Cruyff was the general that everything went through, all 15 goals in the tournament finished or started with him.

Vogts marked him out of the final, literally, which Cruyff protested about at half time, but ref Jack Taylor booked him for complaining. He didn't blossom after that.

O
Opening of the final was held up for 7 minutes because the corner flags were missing. Taylor awarded the first ever penalty in a final, which Holland's' Neeskens scored from in the 2nd minute (no German had touched the ball).

P
Poland conquerors of England made the semi-finals and got 3rd place beating Brazil 1-0. They had to change their tactics pre-tournament, due to the injury to Lubanski, and went with 2 fast wingers and 1 forward. Won 7-0 v Haiti (Szarmach 3). Apparently, sources claim that during their game v Italy, the Italians were offering bribes to the Poles to let them win and go through at the expense of Argentina. Lato was the tournament's top scorer with 7.

Q
Qualifying wise, Holland only got there after a late win v Norway. England missed out; Ramsey was sacked. Haiti qualified mainly because the qualifiers were played on their island. Trinidad & Tobago lost 2-1, after having 4 goals disallowed.

R
Referee Karoly Palotai was an ex international player (Olympics 64), and was now an international ref. Taylor of England became the first to give 2 penalties in a final, the second very debatable; maybe he felt he had to give one the other way. There seemed no contact at all on Holzenbein, who had a reputation for diving.

S
Scotland back for the first time since 1958, were the only unbeaten side in the tournament, and first to be eliminated without losing. Drawing with Brazil and Yugoslavia, but only winning Zaire 2-0 would be there downfall. They went out by 1 goal.

FIFA World Cup A-Z of Facts and Figures

T
Tournament format was changed again, making it like a league, and the more successful teams playing more games in another Round 2 group of games. This contributed to tired players, which deprived the crowd of better games.

U
USSR refused to play the away leg at Santiago stadium due to the fact it was used as a concentration camp for political prisoners after an overthrow of government. Chile qualified through having to kick off against non-opposition.

V
Voodoo taunts pre-tournament by Haiti didn't seem far wrong after going 1-0 up v Italy (ending Zoff's record of 1143 minutes without conceding); they eventually lost 3-1. Tubilandu in goal for Haiti though conceded more goals pro rata than any other keeper.

W
Waterlogged pitch in the semi-final game Poland v W Germany spoilt it for the Poles with their speedy play and wingers, no wonder the Germans wanted it played.

X
Final XI West Germany: Maier, Vogts, Breitner (pen,25), Bonhof, Schwarzenbeck, Beckenbauer (c), Grabowski, Hoeness, **Muller (43),** Overath, Holzenbein
　　　　Holland: Jungbloed, Suubier, Krol, Jansen, Rijsbergen (de Jong 68), Haan, Rep, **Neeskens (pen 2),** van Hanegem, Cruyff, (c), Rensenbrink (R van Kerkhoff HT)

Y
Yugoslavia had 7 different scorers v Zaire a World Cup finals record for an individual game.

Z
Zagallo Brazils coach put together a more physical side to consolidate the European threat. Out injured was Tostao, Clodoaldo

and Carlos Alberto from 1970, in came less flambouyant mediocre players, so the Brazil press said. Still came 3rd, but not good enough for Brazil.

WORLD CUP 1978

ARGENTINA V NETHERLANDS
3-1

FIFA World Cup A-Z of Facts and Figures

TEAM	STANDING	P	W	D	L	F-A
ARGENTINA	CHAMPS	7	5	1	1	15-4
NETHERLANDS	RU	7	3	2	2	15-10
BRAZIL	3RD	7	4	3	0	10-3
ITALY	4TH	7	4	1	2	9-6
POLAND	R2	6	3	1	2	6-6
WEST GERMANY	R2	6	1	4	1	10-5
AUSTRIA	R2	6	3	0	3	7-10
PERU	R2	6	2	1	3	7-12
TUNISIA	R1	3	1	1	1	3-2
SPAIN	R1	3	1	1	1	3-2
SCOTLAND	R1	3	1	1	1	2-2
FRANCE	R1	3	1	0	2	5-5
SWEDEN	R1	3	0	1	2	1-3
IRAN	R1	3	0	1	2	2-8
HUNGARY	R1	3	0	0	3	3-8
MEXICO	R1	3	0	0	3	2-12

FIFA World Cup A-Z of Facts and Figures

A
Argentina win their first World Cup, and on home soil. With a mixture of direct football, lamentable refereeing decisions, and a lot of luck. All their first-round games were played at night, so they knew other results beforehand.

B
Brazil was based in chilly Mor del Plata, more a British climate, which took some acclimatizing to. They got out of their group, just by winning last game 1-0 v Austria (draw would have put them out), but a draw v Argentina 0-0, and not enough goals saw them miss the final on goal difference. They did get 3rd place again though, beating Italy 2-1 (Rivelinos' last international).

C
Cruyff didn't play in the finals; some say because of living in a goldfish bowl environment not to his liking, and maybe also the troubles in Argentina to have an effect? Beckenbauer missing also, due to fact he had gone to ply his trade in USA.

D
Dutch team made the final again but lost for the second successive time to host nation, but a few factors upset their preparations for the final. They were left waiting 10 minutes before kick-off, by the Argentinians, and then they protested about R van Kerkhoffs protective sheaf over his right arm (even though it had been ok in the previous 5 games). Gonella the referee made him bandage it up more before play commenced. Mind games by the Argentinians worked.

E
England failed to qualify again. Their qualifying campaign a disaster, no leadership or direction and Revie quite mid qualifying to take up his post in UAE. 'He picked probably the worst England team ever' in Keegan and Fachetti's words, and lost 2-0, and by the time the calm methodical Greenwood came in, and then beat Italy it was too late.

FIFA World Cup A-Z of Facts and Figures

F
FA of Peru paid speedy winger Munantes' club an insurance premium to make sure they got his services. Peru made the 2nd group stage but finished bottom goalless and pointless. They did top their 1st round group, Cubillas scoring hat trick v Iran, and beating Scotland.

G
General Jorge Rafael Videla dictator of Argentina gave the World Cup to Passerella, with the blood of thousands on his hands. The Mothers of the Plaza de Mayo whose children went missing during his power was pleased the tournament was staged in Argentina, so they could bring the atrocities attention to the world. Junta government seized power before the tournament, nearly throwing it into chaos.

H
Holland's' Ernie Brandts became the first player to score at both ends of the goal in a finals match v Italy 1-2.

I
Israeli referee Avraham Klein, probably the best ref in the world at the time took charge of Italy v Argentina (1st round group game); Italy won 1-0 and kept Argentina's excesses in check. The Argentinians therefore stopped him refereeing any more of their matches in the tournament and had to make do with the 3rd place playoff.

J
Willie **Johnston** of Scotland was sent home in for taking a banned substance, and Dutch journalists laughed and said 'You are pulling my trousers', when they heard that Kenny Burns was the current English Footballer of the Year. They weren't laughing when Scotland beat them 3-2 though.

FIFA World Cup A-Z of Facts and Figures

K
Kimberley de Mar del Plata a local club lent France their green and white striped kit to play in v Hungary, because of a clash of kits on black and white TV, so the game was delayed for 40 minutes.

L
Leopoldo Luque of Argentina brother died in a car accident during the tournament, before they played Italy; Luque understandably declined to play but would go on to score 2 v Peru to help his team reach the final.

M
Menotti; Argentina's coach refused to pick any of Lorenzo's brutal Boca Juniors squad, and wanted to play direct, quick playing football with wingers. The only European based player to play was Kempes, who ended up top scorer in the tournament with 6 goals.

N
Nanninga of Holland has the unfortunate tag of being the first substitute to be sent off in the finals, this for laughing at the referee's decision v W Germany in the 89th minute. First sub to score in a World Cup final.

O
Only 7,938 fans turned up to watch the dismal 1-1 draw between Iran and Scotland. Four days later 35,000 plus turned up to see them beat Holland 3-2, with Gemmill scoring one of the great World Cup goals. They needed to win by 3 clear goals to go through, but again failed.

P
Pitches in numerous new stadiums were laid just before the tournament began, so cut up badly and made big divots. The opening game W Germany v Poland was one such pitch, leading to a now familiar 0-0 score line; the 4th World Cup opener in a row.

Q
Quiroga Peru's goalkeeper was a nationalized Argentinian and let in 6 goals v Argentina in a game, where Argentina had to win by 4 or

more to get to the Final. Bribery and corruption conspiracies enfolded, but nothing came of it. Recent allegations reportedly mention up to £50 million of aid found its way to the Peruvian economy afterwards. Apparently.

R

Rensenbrink of Holland scored the 1000th World Cup finals goal v Scotland from a penalty kick. He also hit the post in the final minute of extra time with the scores at 1-1. Had he scored he would have been top scorer.

S

Scotland one of the pre-tournament favourites was eliminated in the 1st round, they knocked out Czechoslovakia in qualifying too. Manager Ally McLeod declared that they would easily win their group and said, 'My name is McLeod and I am a born winner!' what he lacked in experience as an international manager, he had in abundance in modesty.

T

The **Tickertape** finals has the tournament would be known, as a mass of blue and white descended through the floodlit stadiums. A visual delight. Tunisia became the first African nation to win a finals game; v Mexico 3-1, and kept W Germany to a goalless draw.

U

Unforgettable but vivid was how some summed up the tournament, but off the pitch was where the action was. General Actis the 1st President of the Organizing committee was assassinated when a bomb went off in the press centre before the tournament began.

V

Van der Kerkhoff brothers of Holland were twins, and spookily both scored their only goals of the tournament in different games, but both in the 82nd minute, v Austria and W Germany respectively.

FIFA World Cup A-Z of Facts and Figures

W

West Germany the reigning champions went out in the 2nd round of group games. They were beaten by Austria for the 1st time since 1931, an own goal by Vogts in his last international, and Schoens last game as coach.

X

Final XI Argentina: Fillol, Olguin, Tarantini, gallego, Galván, Passerella (c), **Bertoni (115),** Ardiles (Larossa 65), Luque, **Kempes (37,104),** Ortiz (Houseman 74)

Holland: Jungbloed, Krol (c), Brandts, Poortvliet, Jansen (Suubier 72), Haan, R van der Kerkhoff, Neeskens, Rep **(Nanninga 59), (82),** W van der Kerkhoff, Rensenbrink

Y

Youngest member of Argentina's winning side at aged 23 was Alberto Tarantini; he also became the only player to play in a World Cup final not registered to a club. He had left Boca Jrs before the tournament. Later went on to play for Birmingham City.

Z

Zico of Brazil was part of one of the most farcical incidents of any World Cup. He headed in a corner in the last-minute v Sweden in 1st group game, but whilst the ball was in mid-air, the referee Clive Thomas blew, and disallowed the goal (8 seconds into extra time). Nordqvist of Sweden broke the world record for caps in this game, beating Bobby Moore's 108.

WORLD CUP 1982

ITALY V WEST GERMANY
3-1

FIFA World Cup A-Z of Facts and Figures

TEAM	STANDING	P	W	D	L	F-A
ITALY	CHAMPS	7	4	3	0	12-6
WEST GERMANY	RU	7	3	2	2	12-10
POLAND	SF	7	3	3	1	11-5
FRANCE	SF	7	3	2	2	16-12
BRAZIL	R2	5	4	0	1	15-6
ENGLAND	R2	5	3	2	0	6-1
SOVIET UNION	R2	5	2	2	1	7-4
AUSTRIA	R2	5	2	1	2	5-4
N IRELAND	R2	5	1	3	1	5-7
BELGIUM	R2	5	2	1	2	3-5
ARGENTINA	R2	5	2	0	3	8-7
SPAIN	R2	5	1	2	2	4-5
ALGERIA	R1	3	2	0	1	5-5
HUNGARY	R1	3	1	1	1	12-6
SCOTLAND	R1	3	1	1	1	8-8
YUGOSLAVIA	R1	3	1	1	1	2-2
CAMEROON	R1	3	0	3	0	1-1
HONDURUS	R1	3	0	2	1	2-3
CZECHOSLOVAKIA	R1	3	0	2	1	2-4
PERU	R1	3	0	2	1	2-6
KUWAIT	R1	3	0	1	2	2-6
CHILE	R1	3	0	0	3	3-8
NEW ZEALAND	R1	3	0	0	3	2-12
EL SALVADOR	R1	3	0	0	3	1-13

FIFA World Cup A-Z of Facts and Figures

A

Algeria beat W Germany 2-1, the surprise result of the tournament, and as results stood, going into the last game Germany had to beat Austria to qualify for the next round. They took an early lead, and because both teams were going through; they seemed content in playing the rest of the game out. Fearful furious Algerian fans in the crowd waved money at the players trying, as a ploy to bribe them. This game resulted the last time that final group games were played at different times.

B

Brazil were back at their imperious, flair playing self, scoring magical goals, back heels and shooting from anywhere. Suspect defence was their Achilles heel though. Best team to never win the World Cup. Brazil scored some of the greatest feast of goals ever produced in World Cup history. Eder's flick up volley v USSR, Zico's free-kick v Scotland was top drawer.

C

Carlos Caszely of Chile had the unfortunate honour of being the first player to be sent off and miss a penalty. He was sent off in 1974 v W Germany and missed a penalty v Austria. They lost both games 1-0.

D

Mal **Donaghy** of Northern Ireland became the first British player to be sent off (61 minutes) in the finals v Spain, in a remarkable match. Armstrong had put them 1-0 up after 47 minutes, then the sending off came, and for the last half hour it was like Rourkes Drift for the Irish, but they withheld.

E

England was back after 12 years out, but only just after losing 2 games in qualifying. Bryan Robson after 27 seconds scored the fastest finals goal v France; things were looking good. The team played conservatively and with a lack of direction in the 2nd round games, which saw them go out drawing both games 0-0. The last game England needed to win by 2 goals, struggling they bought on ailing subs Keegan and Brooking, both squandered chances. 27 minutes was there World Cup career, and they were out.

F
Falkland War still unresolved, Argentina came with 9 of the winning squad of '78 and started badly with a loss to Belgium 1-0 in the opening match of the tournament. First goal in opening game for 20 years scored by Vandenbergh.

G
Game of the tournament Italy v Brazil at Sarria, Barcelona. Brazil only needed a draw to go through to the semis, but a hat trick by Rossi (his first goals of the tournament), and suspect defending handed the win to Italy. Italy played the game of their lives, and Brazil just kept coming back with flair and swagger, and in the last minute a header from Oscar was saved on the line by Zoff. Great resilience and luck saw them through.

H
Harold Schumacher keeper of W Germany made the most atrocious, barbaric and now infamous tackles in the history of the World Cup on Patrick Battison of France. Sent through on goal, the keeper came out to the edge of his box and whole body slammed chest high into Battison, knocking him out cold, and he lost numerous teeth. The referee awarded a goal kick, and no booking!!! Later Schumacher offered to pay to have them capped.

I
Italy became World Champions for the 3rd time, after a slow start where they drew all their opening group games. A solid defence, with strong 'cattacio' methods and even stronger tackling got them their rewards. Pre-tournament scandal involving match fixing scandals in Serie 'A' seemed to gel the squad together throughout their campaign.

J
John Adshead the New Zealand coach was English and was unlucky being drawn in a tough group. They lost every game scored 2 and

conceded 12. In the qualifiers they had Wilson in goal, and conceded 0 goals, then for the finals they went with van Huttum??

K
Kuwait v France had a farcical moment when, Giresse scored a goal, but the Kuwaiti players had stopped because they heard a whistle (from the crowd). Sheik Al-Sabah their general manager ordered the players off the pitch in protest. They only came back on when Stuper the referee disallowed the goal; he never refereed another finals game after this. Kuwait was fined £6,500 for their antics, small change for the oil rich nation.

L
Laszlo Kiss of Hungary became the first substitute to score a hat trick, and the fastest (33 minutes) in their emphatic destroying of El Salvador 10-1 (highest score in the finals). This in front of just 6,000 fans.

M
Diego **Maradona** made his World Cup bow v Belgium (lost 1-0 but hit the bar). Menotti thought him to young in 1978 at 17. His first finals goal was v Hungary, he scored 2. He got sent off v Brazil in the 2nd group round for retaliation in a frustrating game for him. He was kicked, bumped and shirt pulled all game v Italy by man marking Gentile (media had a separate camera on him throughout the game). Maradona's time would come next tournament.

N
Northern Ireland was the best British team in the finals, they beat the host nation Spain to progress into the next round, where they finished bottom of the group. It could all have been different if O'Neill's early goal had been allowed v France. Norman Whiteside was the youngest player to ever play in the finals at the age of 17 years and 41 days. Healy was the only player from an Irish club (Coleraine) to ever play in the finals.

O
Organization of the tournament was perilous. Britain was at war with Argentina, and Poland and El Salvador were in turmoil. Spain perennially threatened by the terrorism of Basque separatists and feared withdrawing from the greatest show on Earth.

P
Paolo Rossi was back after a 2-year ban for involvement for match fixing, ended up the top scorer with 6 goals. All coming in the last 3 games.

Q
Qualifying saw 3 British teams qualify, but again no Uruguay, and the past 2 tournament finalists Holland missing. Honduras qualified from CONCACAF sections final round in their own country. New Zealand beat Fiji 13-0 in their qualifiers.

R
Karl- Heinz **Rumminigge** wasn't fully fit for the final, but played (to Stielike's disgust), but still finished up with 5 goals, including a hat trick v Chile, a class forward and current European Footballer of the Year.

S
Semi-final W Germany v France was the first game ever to be decided on penalties in a World Cup finals Germany won 5-4, after a 3-3 draw after extra time. France were 3-1 up with only 17 minutes left, before the Germans never say die attitude won the day. Bossis missed the decisive penalty.

T
'Tim' Peru's coach was the oldest ever to coach a team at the finals at 67 years of age. He also represented Brazil in 1938 finals v Czechoslovakia. When Peru played Cameroon, Tim came up against their French coach Vincent who also played in the finals in 1954 and 58.

U
Uruguayan Jose Santamaria was host nation Spain's' coach for the tournament. Lacking a quality striker, they struggled to get past the 2nd group stage, going out in England's group.

V
Venue for the final was the Bernabeau in Madrid where over 90,000 fans saw Italy victorious, but only after the first ever missed penalty in a final by Antonio Cabrini of Italy, who scuffed it wide. Altobelli was the first sub to be subbed in a final.

W
West Germany qualified strongly scoring 33 goals and conceding only 3. Their enigmatic maestro Schuster was missing through injury, but their resolute, dogged German mentality got them through to the final were their luck ran out, losing to Italy after they scored a quick-fire 3 goals in 17 minutes in the final.

X
Final XI: Italy: Zoff (c), Bergomi, Cabrini, Gentile, Oriali, Collovatti, Scirea, **Tardelli (68),** Conti, **Rossi (56),** Graziani (**Altobelli (7), (80,)** Causio (89)

West Germany: Schumacher, Kaltz, Briegal, B Forster, KH Forster, Stielike, Littbarski, Dremmler (Hrubbesch 62), **Brietner (83),** Fischer, Rumminigge (c) (H Muller 70)

Y
Yet again the format of the tournament was tampered with. This time there were 24 teams that made up the finals, and they were split up into 6 groups of 4, with the top 2 from each group going into another round of groups. Round 2 groups were made up of 3 teams in 4 groups, with the top teams making the semi-finalists.

Z
Dino **Zoff** became the oldest ever player and captain to lift the World Cup at the age of 40 years and 133 days. He also played his 100th international v Poland during the finals.

WORLD CUP 1986

ARGENTINA V WEST GERMANY
3-2

FIFA World Cup A-Z of Facts and Figures

TEAM	STANDING	P	W	D	L	F-A
ARGENTINA	CHAMPS	7	6	1	0	14-5
WEST GERMANY	RU	7	3	2	2	8-7
FRANCE	SF	7	4	2	1	12-6
BELGIUM	SF	7	2	2	3	12-15
BRAZIL	QF	5	4	1	0	10-1
MEXICO	QF	5	3	2	0	6-2
SPAIN	QF	5	3	1	1	11-4
ENGLAND	QF	5	2	1	2	7-3
DENMARK	R2	4	3	0	1	10-6
SOVIET UNION	R2	4	2	1	1	12-5
MOROCCO	R2	4	1	2	1	3-2
ITALY	R2	4	1	2	1	5-6
PARAGUAY	R2	4	1	2	1	4-6
POLAND	R2	4	1	1	2	1-7
BULGARIA	R2	4	0	2	2	2-6
URUGUAY	R2	4	0	2	2	2-8
PORTUGAL	R1	3	1	0	2	2-4
HUNGARY	R1	3	1	0	2	2-9
SCOTLAND	R1	3	0	1	2	1-3
SOUTH KOREA	R1	3	0	1	2	4-7
N IRELAND	R1	3	0	1	2	2-6
ALGERIA	R1	3	0	1	2	1-5
IRAQ	R1	3	0	0	3	1-4
CANADA	R1	3	0	0	3	0-5

FIFA World Cup A-Z of Facts and Figures

A
Argentina became the 2nd nation to win the World Cup out of their continent. Many regarded Diego Maradona did it almost single handed. He scored 5 goals, and set up more, on their run to winning the trophy. Scoring the 'Goal of the Century, and 'Hand of God' goals v England in the Quarters being the major highlight of the finals. Marco Trobbiani has the shortest finals appearance on record to date, coming on as substitute for 1 minute.

B
Belgium made the semi-finals for the 1st time, even after finishing 3rd in their group, but lost to Argentina 2-0. Enzo Scifo their playmaker turned down Italy to play for them and was their best player. Gerets played despite being guilty in a bribery case. Their 7 goal 2nd round game thriller v USSR lit up the tournament (4-3).

C
Canada the part timers made their 1st, and up to now only appearance in the finals. They were coached by former England international keeper Tony Walters. They went out in the 1st round without scoring.

D
Denmark was finalists for the 1st time, and had an exciting team, and one of the pre-tournament favourites. A magnificent win v Uruguay 6-1 (Elkjear 3), was followed by a not so great 5-1 drubbing by Spain.

E
England got through to the knockout stage; just, by beating Poland in their last group game. Eventually lost to Argentina 2-1. Kerry Dixon has the record of shortest finals career for an England player, to date (6 minutes).

F
France was knocked out in the semi-finals again by W Germany for the 2nd tournament running. Tendonitis hampered Platini throughout the tournament and wasn't the player who captained them to Euro glory 2 years earlier. They knocked out a strong Brazil team in the quarters on penalties, but only after Zico had missed one in normal

time, just after coming on as sub. Zico and Socrates's last games for Brazil.

G
Gary Lineker of England was the top scorer with 6 goals, 3 of which came against Poland. The last goal in the 3-0-win v Paraguay was the 1,300th World Cup goal.

H
Joao **Havelange** FIFA president kept to 24 qualifiers to really appease Africa and Asia contingent who provided his power base. Corruption, bribery and power were the way he ran FIFA, and he normally got what he wanted.

I
Injury to Bryan Robson's shoulder and a sending off, Ray Wilkins being the first England player to have this accolade for throwing the ball at the referees feet v Morocco, after being booked probably made coach Robson change tactics, dropping the winger and target man approach, but had to bring it back, maybe too late in the final minutes of the game v Argentina.

J
Pat **Jennings** of Northern Ireland retired after his last, and World Recorded 119th game v Brazil. They lost 3-1, with a stunner from Josimar. All on his 41st birthday.

K
Khairi of Morocco was only on the field 27 seconds before the final whistle was blown after coming on as sub v Poland (a finals record). He also scored 2 v Portugal to help Morocco become the first African nation to qualify for the next round and win a group. Beaten by West Germany 1-0 with 2 minutes to go.

L
Lobanovsky USSR's coach was also the manager of Dynamo Kiev, a coach driven by regimental tactics and supreme fitness, his squad was

ready for the demands of playing at altitude and in the heat. 9 of his first team v Hungary in their 6-0 opener played for Kiev.

M
Mexico became the first country to stage the finals twice, despite a devastating earthquake 8 months prior to the tournament starting. Original choice Colombia had to withdraw because of financial and economic difficulties. Hugo Sanchez and Co got to the quarter finals before losing to W Germany 4-1 on penalties, in an ill-tempered game with 7 yellows and 2 red.

N
Notts County had an unlikely representative in the form of Rachid Harkouk of Algeria, who didn't get through the group stage.

O
Organizers of the tournament bowed down to TV companies. Guillermo Canedo, a leading executive with a Mexican TV company, insisted on staging games in the middle of the day when temperatures were at their highest, and games had to be finished on the dot to satisfy TV deadline. Probably deals were struck by Havelange and Televista to satisfy each other's needs.

P
Paraguay's coach Re became the first coach ever to be sent off in the World Cup finals, in the game v Belgium, 5 minutes from the end.

Q
Qualifying saw 3 British teams there again, Scotland qualified by beating Australia in a playoff. A record 120 entries for the competition, with the top 2 from each European group with 5 teams automatically qualifying. Argentina qualified despite losing and drawing v Peru.

R
Ramon Caldere of Spain scored 2 v Algeria and was then found to have taken the stimulant ephedrine at a hospital for gastric problems. He escaped punishment, but the team doctor was told off, and the

Spanish FA cautioned. Spain got through to the quarter finals losing to Belgium 5-4 on penalties. This after hammering Denmark 5-1 with Butragueno scoring 4.

S
Scotland's coach Jock Stein died of a heart attack before the tournament started during a 1-1 drawing qualifier v Wales. Alex Ferguson took over the duties but was knocked out again in the group stages. Going into the last game needing a win to see them through, even after losing their first 2 games, they drew 0-0 against a Uruguayan team that had Batista sent off in the 1st minute. In the finals they only managed a miserable 7 shots on target.

T
Tournament format changed yet again. 24 teams had to be whittled down to 16 for the knockout stages, ousting a 2nd group stage. So, group winners and runners up went through out of the 6 groups, and the best 4 third place teams, made up the 16.

U
Uruguay were back in the World Cup after 14 years out, despite only drawing 2 of their group games went through and had 2 men sent off in final 2 group games, plus Batista V Scotland. The bad boys were back alright. Argentina knocked them out 1-0 in the last 16.

V
Venue for the final was the Azteca stadium that held over 120,000 fans and has been the most used stadium per games than any other in the history of the World Cup. The Mexican Wave a phenomenon during the finals, where everyone in turn around the stadium stood up and waved in continuation was an amazing sight to see.

W
West Germany had Beckenbauer as their coach, Schuster refused to play this time, but they still made the final again. Beckenbauer nearly became the second coach/player to win the cup, he said that his team was too young, and stood a better chance in 4 years' time.

Rumminigge became the first player to captain 2 World Cup final teams to defeat.

X
Final XI: Argentina: Pumpido, Cuciuffo, Olarticoechea, Enrique, Ruggeri, **Brown (23),** Giusti, Batista, **Burruchaga (85),** Trobbiani 89, Maradona (c), **Valdano (56)**

West Germany: Schumacher, Berthold, Briegel, Jakobs, Forster kh, Eder, Matthaus, Brehme, Allofs (**Voller 46 HT 82),** Magath (Hoeness 61), **Rumminigge (c)(74)**

Y
Yugoslavian Boro Milutinovic coached host nation Mexico to the quarter finals.

Z
Zmuda of Brazil was bought on as a sub v Poland so he could equal Seelers 21 finals appearances a world record at the time.

FIFA World Cup A-Z of Facts and Figures

WORLD CUP 1990

WEST GERMANY V ARGENTINA
1-0

FIFA World Cup A-Z of Facts and Figures

TEAM	STANDING	P	W	D	L	F-A
WEST GERMANY	CHAMPS	7	5	2	0	15-5
ARGENTINA	RU	7	2	3	2	5-4
ITALY	SF	7	6	1	0	10-2
ENGLAND	SF	7	3	3	1	8-6
YUGOSLAVIA	QF	5	3	1	1	8-6
CZECHOSLOVAKIA	QF	5	3	0	2	10-5
CAMEROON	QF	5	3	0	2	7-9
REP OF IRELAND	QF	5	0	4	1	2-3
BRAZIL	R2	4	3	0	1	4-2
SPAIN	R2	4	2	1	1	6-4
BELGIUM	R2	4	2	0	2	6-4
ROMANIA	R2	4	1	2	1	4-3
COSTA RICA	R2	4	2	0	2	4-6
COLOMBIA	R2	4	1	1	2	4-4
NETHERLANDS	R2	4	0	3	1	3-4
URUGUAY	R2	4	1	1	2	2-5
SOVIET UNION	R1	3	1	0	2	4-4
AUSTRIA	R1	3	1	0	2	2-3
SCOTLAND	R1	3	1	0	2	2-3
EGYPT	R1	3	0	1	2	1-2
SWEDEN	R1	3	0	0	3	3-6
SOUTH KOREA	R1	3	0	0	3	1-6
USA	R1	3	0	0	3	2-8
UAE	R1	3	0	0	3	2-11

FIFA World Cup A-Z of Facts and Figures

A
Argentina had their main man Maradona leading them to the final. A bad build up to the tournament with 1 win in 10 v Israel didn't look good, and with Maradona suffering a swollen foot, with an inflamed toenail; things were tough! They beat their main rivals Brazil 1-0, and Italy on penalties on way to final. 2 bookings for their main player Caniggia, meant he missed the final. First team not to score in a WORLD CUP final.

B
Brazil had a strong defence but lacked a midfield maestro. They missed star striker Romario with a broken leg prior to tournament and lacked the fire power in games only scoring 4 goals in 4 games, even though creating 50 plus chances. Out to rivals Argentina in round of 16; 1-0.

C
Cameroon beat the reigning champions Argentina in the opening game 1-0 and had 2 players sent off in separate incidents on Caniggia. They topped the group and lost for the first time in 6 WORLD CUP games in the game v USSR, who was eliminated. Cameroon went on to give England a fright in the Quarter finals before being narrowly beaten 3-2. First African nation to get to Quarters.

D
The **Dutch** were back in the WORLD CUP for first time since 1978 and were reigning European Champions. They drew all 3 group games and qualified in 3rd place. They met their rivals W Germany in the next round and lost an ill-tempered game 2-1.

E
England made the semi-finals for the first time on foreign soil. They topped their group, beat Belgium in the next round with a last-minute goal in extra time from David Platt. Beat a spirited Cameroon next, before a nerve-racking semi-final loss to W Germany on penalties after a 1-1 draw.

FIFA World Cup A-Z of Facts and Figures

F
Final four teams left in completion were all previous winners with 8 WORLD CUP's to their names. This is the second time this has happened 1970 being the other.

G
Paul **Gascoigne** England's best player got booked in the semi, which meant he would have missed the final if England got there. Tears followed, an iconic image of these finals.

H
Rene **Higuita** Colombia's flamboyant and eccentric goalkeeping finally cost his team, when he rushed out of goal trying to take on a Cameroon player, lost the ball and conceded a goal. They lost the match and were knocked out. He would miss the next finals due to being imprisoned for charges of kidnapping.

I
Italy was the first European team to host the tournament twice. Strong defence. They finished 3rd after beating England, they won 6 games in the tournament drawing the other, whilst Argentina got to the final winning just 2 games.

J
Jubilant Franz Beckenbauer became the first player to both captain and coach a WORLD CUP winning team. Zagello of Brazil is the only other to have done this, but he wasn't captain. It was also the first time a team from UEFA won the final against a non-European team.

K
Keeper Peter Shilton kept his 10th WORLD CUP finals clean sheet, a record v Belgium. Also, he became the oldest captain in WORLD CUP history at 40 years 292 days, and broke Pat Jennings caps record of 119 games in the game v Italy.

L
Long ball specialists Republic of Ireland made their first appearance at finals. Under Jack Charlton, they used this tactic to their best ability, even though not great to watch, and the ball in the England game only being in play for 49 minutes it paid dividends. They progressed through the group stages, and then beat Romania on penalties, before coming unstuck against the Italians in the Quarters, Eire's best performance to date in a WORLD CUP.

M
Pedro **Monzon** of Argentina became the first player ever to be sent off in a WORLD CUP final. It was in the 68th minute for a foul on Klinsmann. He was later followed by his teammate Dezzotti (86th minute) for grabbing Vollers throat.

N
Nine bookings in the Austria v USA (5 Aus, 4 USA) game set an at the time unwanted record for a finals match. Aigner of Austria was also sent off.

O
Oldest player to score in a finals match was Roger Milla of Cameroon, who was reported to be 38 years of age (dispute due to no birth certificate). He went on to score 4 in total, not bad for a player who was playing his club football for a team called Reunion on an island in the Indian Ocean.

P
Pumpido Argentina's goalkeeper broke his leg in the game v USSR, his replacement Goycochea was in inspired form especially in penalty shoot outs where he saved 2 penalties in each of the games v Yugoslavia and Italy.

Q
Qualifying consisted of 112 nations. England didn't concede a goal, Holland and Germany qualified from same group. Colombia qualified

as worst group winners by points in S America then beat Israel in a playoff for the finals. 24 teams qualified.

R
More **red** cards were shown in this WORLD CUP than any other, to date, totalling 16. Also, this had the lowest goal per game ratio of any WORLD CUP (2.21), something had to change.

S
Sardinia in Sicily was the place used to 'house' the football hooligans of England. All England's group games were played here.

T
Toto Schillaci of Italy was the WORLD CUP's top scorer with 6 goals. His first ever international goal came in the game v Austria that set him on his way to Italian folklore.

U
United Arab Emirates, who were coached by Carlos Alberto Perreira of Brazil, were knocked out in the group stages, not surprising given only 3000 registered players. Fielded 2 sets of brother's v Colombia.

V
Rudi **Voller** and Frank Rijkaard were both sent off in an ill-tempered game between W Germany and Holland. Rijkaard after fouling Voller disgustingly spat on him, and Voller in disbelief remonstrated with him, and dually got himself sent off. As they were walking off the pitch, Rijkaard jogged past Rudi and spat on him again in the hair. In the final it was a foul on Voller that led to the penalty being scored to win the final.

W
West Germany became champions for the 3rd time after Brehme scored a penalty to win the game 1-0 v Argentina. Revenge for 4 years earlier. He was left back and scored the penalty with his right foot. A very attacking team full of flair and grit had some support in

Italy due to players playing over there. This was their 3rd final in a row, 3rd time lucky.

X
Final XI West Germany: Illgner, Bertold (Reuter), Kohler, Augenthaler, Buchwald, **Brehme (85pen)**, Littbarski, Hassler, Matthaus (c), Voller, Klinsmann

Argentina: Goycochea, Lorenzo, Serrizuela, Sensini, Ruggeri (Monzón), Simón, Basualdo, Burruchaga (Calderón), Maradona (c), Troglio, Dezotti

Y
Yugoslavian coach Milutinovic now was coach of Costa Rica who made it to the 2nd round becoming the first Central American team to win a match in Europe v Scotland 1-0, also beat Sweden 2-1. Eventually lost to Czechoslovakia 4-1, and 3 Scuhravy headed goals.

Z
Walter **Zenga** Italy's goalkeeper went a record 517 minutes without conceding a goal, until Maradona scored against him on Maradona's home pitch in Napoli.

WORLD CUP 1994

BRAZIL V ITALY
0-0 (3-2 PENS)

FIFA World Cup A-Z of Facts and Figures

TEAM	STANDING	P	W	D	L	F-A
BRAZIL	CHAMPS	7	5	2	0	11-3
ITALY	RU	7	4	2	1	8-5
SWEDEN	SF	7	3	3	1	15-8
BULGARIA	SF	7	3	1	3	10-11
GERMANY	QF	5	3	1	1	9-7
ROMANIA	QF	5	3	1	1	10-9
NETHERLANDS	QF	5	3	0	2	8-6
SPAIN	QF	5	2	2	1	10-6
NIGERIA	R2	4	2	0	2	7-4
ARGENTINA	R2	4	2	0	2	8-6
BELGIUM	R2	4	2	0	2	4-4
SAUDI ARABIA	R2	4	2	0	2	5-6

FIFA World Cup A-Z of Facts and Figures

MEXICO	R2	4	1	2	1	4-4
USA	R2	4	1	1	2	3-4
SWITZERLAND	R2	4	1	1	2	5-7
REP OF IRELAND	R2	4	1	1	2	2-4
NORWAY	R1	3	1	1	1	1-1
RUSSIA	R1	3	1	0	2	7-6
COLOMBIA	R1	3	1	0	2	4-5
SOUTH KOREA	R1	3	0	2	1	4-5
BOLIVIA	R1	3	0	1	2	1-4
CAMEROON	R1	3	0	1	2	3-11
MOROCCO	R1	3	0	0	3	2-5
GREECE	R1	3	0	0	3	0-10

FIFA World Cup A-Z of Facts and Figures

A
Argentina had to qualify via playoff v Australia, bringing back Maradona to see them through. A great start to WORLD CUP beating Greece 4-0 with Batistuta getting 3, and Maradona getting the other. He was later banned from the tournament for testing positive for banned substances. He had the most appearances as captain at any WORLD CUP in this campaign, 16 games.

B
Brazil became champions for the 4th time, without their regular centre half, but had a great attack in Romario and Bebeto. A downside to their victory came when Leonardo got sent off for a blatant elbow on Ramos of USA and fracturing his skull. They beat Holland in a scintillating quarter final 3-2. Won the final 3-2 on penalties after the first 0-0 in a final.

C
Colombia was pre-tournament favourites but finished bottom of their group. They had death threats against players, and 8 days after losing to the USA, poor Andres Escobar was murdered in Medellin, shot dead. Allegedly due to a bet that went wrong, and someone losing a lot of money.

D
Dahlin of Sweden became the first coloured player to represent them at finals, and helped them to the semi-finals, before losing narrowly to Brazil 1-0.

E
England didn't qualify, after a disastrous qualifying campaign (Gualteiri of San Marino scored fastest qualifying goal ever after 8 seconds). The only British representatives were Rep of Ireland. The same long ball tactics upset Italy in their first game which Ireland won 1-0; their first finals win. Aldridge became the oldest British player to score in the finals at 35 years 279 days v Mexico

FIFA World Cup A-Z of Facts and Figures

F
French referee Joel Quiniou sent off most players overall in WORLD CUP history with 5; 3 in this WORLD CUP and 22 yellows respectively.

G
Germany was now a united nation again but had an aging squad. They were the first team to get 3pts for a win by beating Bolivia 1-0 in the opening game. Etcheverry of Bolivia got sent off after 4 minutes.

H
Havelange the FIFA president again scheduled games in the hottest part of the day in high heat and humidity. He banned Pelé from the opening ceremony for criticising head of Brazilian FA Teixeira (Havelange's son in law).

I
Italy made it to the final again on a sound strong defence but lacked strike force. Injuries hampered them throughout the tournament, having to patch players up like Baresi (played the first and last game of tournament, had a knee operation in between), and Baggio as the WORLD CUP unfolded. Baggio scored 5 goals in the knockout stages.

J
Jack Charlton Ireland coach was caught on camera shouting and swearing at officials during the Mexico game for not allowing drink breaks in the stifling heat, this wasn't true, all he had to do was go on the touchline. He got a 1 match ban and £1,000 fine. They lost last 16 game to Holland 2-0 and were knocked out.

K
A **kiss** on the post by keeper Pagliuca after the ball slipped through his hands from a shot by Marcio Santos in the WORLD CUP final. Relieved and affectionate. Pagliuca also became the first keeper to be sent off in the history of WORLD CUP in the group game v Norway for a reckless tackle on Leonardsson.

L
Los Angeles' Pasadena Rose Bowl was the venue of the final attracting 94,194 to the game.

M
Michel Frances' coach in 1986 was now Cameroon coach. They threatened to boycott game v Brazil due to unpaid bonuses in qualifying. They did play and got beat 3-0. Pagal a player from 1990 was omitted from squad by Michel, when he found out he smacked someone in the face at the airport.

N
Player's **names** were put on the back of their shirts for the first time in this WORLD CUP.

O
Oldest player to score in a WORLD CUP extending his record from 1990 was Roger Milla at 42, who scored v Russia (1-6). Youngest player to be sent off in WORLD CUP history was Rigobert Song at 17 years 358 days v Brazil. Just over 25 years between them.

P
Penalties were the outcome for the final, the first time this has happened. The first 2 were missed, by Baresi and Marcia Santos. Then Albertini and Evani for Italy, and Romario and Branco scored for Brazil. Tafferel then saved Massaro's, and captain Dunga scored for Brazil. Up stepped the 'Divine Ponytail' Roberto Baggio, Italy's poster boy to try and save his team. Unfortunately, his weary shot blasted over the bar. Brazil was champions. Diana Ross also opened the WORLD CUP with a pre-planned penalty that when scored split a goal in two; the goal split, but Ross missed the goal!!

Q
Qualification consisted of 143 teams; France missed out losing their last 2 games. Greece Nigeria and Saudi Arabia were there for the first time. England missed out finishing 3rd in their group. Russia competed as an independent country after the dissolution of the

Soviet Union. East and West Germany were unified for the first time since 1938 WORLD CUP. Africa was given 3 spots for the first time. Czechoslovakia competed as 'Representation of Czechs and Slovaks (RCS) after 1992 dissolution. Chile still suspended from 1990 WORLD CUP for interruption of game v Brazil in 1990 qualifying.

R
Some of **Russia's'** players earlier in their season went to their Minister of Sport asking for the coach Sadyrin to be sacked, he stayed, but 7 rebels were left out of the squad. The team was knocked out in the group stages despite a 6-1-win v Cameroon, where Salenko scored 5 goals in the game; a record. Sergei Gorlukovich equalled the fastest caution in a WORLD CUP finals game vs Sweden in the 1st minute (equal with Marini (Italy v Poland 1982).

S **Switzerland** was coached by Englishman Roy Hodgson in their first finals since 1966. Their match v USA in The Pontiac Silverdome, Detroit was the first indoor game ever in a WORLD CUP. They got out of their group but lost to Spain in the next round 3-0. In 22 WORLD CUP finals games they have never kept a clean sheet.

T
Tournament firsts included meetings between 2 Arab countries (S Arabia v Morocco 2-1) and allowing of 3 substitutes in a game if a goalkeeper is injured (Morocco 1st team to do this). Top scorers in the tournament were Sweden with 15 goals, got beat 1-0 in semi v Brazil.

U
USA hosted the tournament, the first time it had been held out of Europe and S America. It topped the charts for best attendances, and goals to game ratio (2.71) at any previous WORLD CUPs, less policing at games and best stadiums. An average team that got to 2nd round losing to Brazil 1-0. Clavijo became the oldest player to be sent off in the finals of a WORLD CUP at 37 years of age v USA.

V
Bertie **Vogts** Germanys coach sent home Steffen Effenberg for a one fingered gesture to his own fans after their game v S Korea, and never played under Vogts again. Germany got beat in an enthralling quarter final v Bulgaria, losing 2-1. Bulgaria's goals coming in the last 15 minutes.

W
Wins for Bulgaria came in this WORLD CUP after 17 consecutive defeats, stretching back to 1962. Their first v Greece 4-0 in the group stage. A win on penalties v Mexico saw a quarter final encounter and victory v Germany, which set up a first semi-final for them v Italy. Unfortunately, a game too far for the gallant Bulgarians where they lost to a Baggio inspired Italy 2-1. Their world class striker Stoichkov was joint top scorer of the WORLD CUP with Salenko with 6 goals.

X
Final XI: Brazil: Taffarel, Jorghino (Cafu 21), Marcio Santos, Aldair, Branco, Mazinho, Mauro Silva, Dunga, Zinho (Viola 106), Bebeto, Romario

Italy: Pagliuca, Mussi (Apolloni 34), Maldini, Baresi, Benarrivo, Donadoni, Albertini, Baggio D (Evani 95), Berti, Baggio R, Massaro

Y
Yugoslavia was suspended form international competition from 1992-4, so unable to qualify due to war in Bosnia and splitting up of country, Greece was their replacement. Yugoslav representation was there by means of coach Milutonivic who coached USA; his 3rd different team at a WORLD CUP.

Z
Gianfranco **Zola** of Italy was controversially sent off after only being on the pitch for 12 minutes v Nigeria, and on his 28th birthday too.

WORLD CUP 1998

FRANCE V BRAZIL
3-0

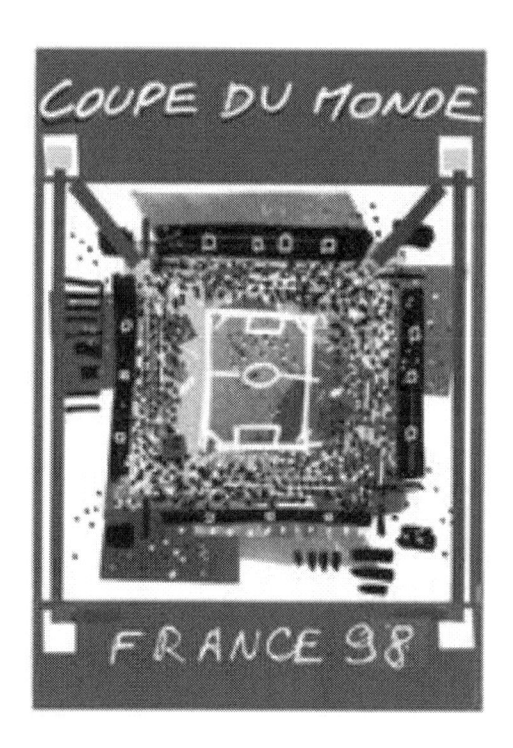

FIFA World Cup A-Z of Facts and Figures

TEAM	STANDING	P	W	D	L	F-A
FRANCE	CHAMPS	7	6	1	0	15-2
BRAZIL	RU	7	4	1	2	14-10
CROATIA	SF	7	5	0	2	11-5
NETHERLANDS	SF	7	3	3	1	13-7
ITALY	QF	5	3	2	0	8-3
ARGENTINA	QF	5	3	1	1	10-4
GERMANY	QF	5	3	1	1	8-6
DENMARK	QF	5	2	1	2	9-7
ENGLAND	R2	4	2	1	1	7-4
YUGOSLAVIA	R2	4	2	1	1	5-4
ROMANIA	R2	4	2	1	1	4-3
NIGERIA	R2	4	2	0	2	6-9
MEXICO	R2	4	1	2	1	8-7
PARAGUAY	R2	4	1	2	1	3-2
NORWAY	R2	4	1	2	1	5-5
CHILE	R2	4	0	3	1	5-8
SPAIN	R1	3	1	1	1	8-4
MOROCCO	R1	3	1	1	1	5-5
BELGIUM	R1	3	0	3	0	3-3
IRAN	R1	3	1	0	2	2-4
COLOMBIA	R1	3	1	0	2	1-3
JAMAICA	R1	3	1	0	2	3-9
AUSTRIA	R1	3	0	2	1	3-4
SOUTH AFRICA	R1	3	0	2	1	3-6
CAMEROON	R1	3	0	2	1	2-5
TUNISIA	R1	3	0	1	2	1-4
SCOTLAND	R1	3	0	1	2	2-6
SAUDI ARABIA	R1	3	0	1	2	2-7
BULGARIA	R1	3	0	1	2	1-7
SOUTH KOREA	R1	3	0	1	2	2-9
JAPAN	R1	3	0	0	3	1-4
USA	R1	3	0	0	3	1-5

FIFA World Cup A-Z of Facts and Figures

A
The **Azzuri** (Italy) reached the Quarter finals before bowing out to France 4-3 on penalties. This was Italy's 3rd WORLD CUP in a row they have been knocked out on penalties; coach Cesere Maldini says they are cursed!! Maldini also managed his son Paulo who was in the squad.

B
'**Bafana Bafana**'; South Africa made their debut WORLD CUP; they lost all 3 games. Issa scored 2 own goals v France (6 scored overall in the tournament; a record), and the 1-1 draw v Denmark saw 3 men get sent off (2 Danes, 1 S Africa, all subs).

C
Jose Luis **Chilavert** Paraguay's eccentric keeper, and scorer of 41 international goals, nearly added to his tally in the game v Bulgaria, but his free kick was tipped over. He led his team out of the group conceding 1 goal, and nearly kept out France in the next round losing 1-0 in extra time.

D
Denmark reached the quarter finals beating Nigeria in the last 16, with a goal from Ebbe Sand 16 seconds after coming on as a substitute, making it the fastest goal from a sub. Michael Laudrup holds the record for the longest period between 1st and last finals goal with 12 years 16 days.

E
England made it out of the group and faced Argentina in round of 16 in a classic encounter. A wonder goal from 18-year-old Owen, 2 penalties in the first 10 minutes, England disallowed goal when down to 10 men and David Beckham getting himself sent off. Beckham's petulant kick out after being fouled by Simeone got him his marching orders on 47 minutes left a back to the walls, bulldog England performance that nearly paid off. England eventually lost 4-3 on penalties after a 2-2 draw.

F
France won their first WORLD CUP as hosts (for the 2nd time). Played with an average out of sort's striker in Guivarch, who didn't score in the tournament. Coasted through the group stages, beat Italy on penalties after 0-0 in the quarters. In the semi-final they beat a spirited Croatia 2-1, with Lillian Thurams first ever international goals in over 50 caps. The final saw France beat Brazil 3-0, Brazil's worst defeat in the finals since 1930. Desailly was sent off with 20 minutes to go. France topped the goal scoring charts with 15 goals.

G
The **golden goal** was introduced in this WORLD CUP and was first used in the game France v Paraguay, where Blanc scored in the 114th minute. The only golden goal of the tournament.

H
Holland reached the semi-finals, where after 1-1 score line they were knocked out on penalties 4-2. Off field relationships were strained, Edger Davids and coach Guus Hiddink didn't see eye to eye, and a bust up between Van der Sar and Bogarde came to blows. Technically brilliant, but team ethic all wrong. A great win in the quarter's v Argentina 2-1 with a last-minute wonder goal by Bergkamp their highlight of the WORLD CUP. Finished in 4th place losing to Croatia 2-1.

I
Iran v USA was a match that stoked up a lot of political emotions between these two warring nations. Both teams came out with flowers for each other as a goodwill gesture, and played an enthralling game which Iran won 2-1, and knocked out their political enemy with an 84th min goal by Mahdavikia. Iran need to beat Germany in their last game to progress but lost 2-0.

J
Japan and Jamaica made their WORLD CUP debuts, both eliminated in the same group. Jamaica won the match 2-1 between each other. Robbie Earle of the premiership scored Jamaica's first ever WORLD

FIFA World Cup A-Z of Facts and Figures

CUP goal. Japan now looks forward to co-hosting 2002 WORLD CUP.

K
Henryk **Kasperczak** Tunisia's Polish coach was sacked after 2 games, which mattered not has they were eliminated from the group after 2 losses.

L
Leider Preciado the scorer of Colombia's winner v Tunisia 1-0, was the survivor of a tidal wave which swept through his village when he was younger.

M
Mario Zagello in his 3rd finals as Brazilian coach, nearly won a second WORLD CUP in charge, but fell at the final hurdle. The build-up was extraordinary as he sent in the team sheet minus star player Ronaldo, who in the minutes building up to start had a convulsion type of fit, so Zagello put Edmundo in his starting line-up. 15 minutes later he had reversed the decision, as Ronaldo was reinstated, but his pre match health problems hindered his performance.

N
New president of FIFA Sepp Blatter oversaw his first finals, and new rules he introduced were the golden goal, banning tackling from behind and allowing 3 substitutes per game. Also kept 3 points for a win instead of 2.

O
4th **officials** in this WORLD CUP used electronic scoreboards instead of cardboard ones for the first time.

P
Robert **Prosinecki** of Croatia became the first person to score for 2 different teams at WORLD CUP's, when he scored v Jamaica. This added to his goal in 1990 for Yugoslavia v UAE

FIFA World Cup A-Z of Facts and Figures

Q
32 teams **qualified** for the finals for the first time. 8 groups of 4 teams, with the top 2 from each group going through to a straightforward knockout format. 174 teams entered; a record. 4 teams debuted; Jamaica, Japan, Croatia and South Africa. Scotland qualified again, but for their 8th finals running still didn't make it out of the group. Iran qualified by beating Australia over 2 legs.

R
Referee for the final Said Belqola from Morocco was the first African to referee the final. Linesman Marc Warren was from England. A record 22 red cards were given out in the tournament, and Rigobert Song became the first player to be sent off in 2 different finals. Laurent Blanc missed the final having got sent off in the semi v Croatia.

S
Skipper of the Germans; Lother Mathaus played in a record 25th finals match, and his last finals game v Croatia; a record. Also, his 5th finals.

T
Top scorer in the WORLD CUP was Davor Suker of debutants Croatia with 6 goals. Finished in 3rd place which is a joint record for a team debuting with Portugal 1966.

U
Unbelievably Paul Gascoigne was omitted from the final 23-man squad for England, even after his immense performance in qualifying v Italy, where England got the draw they needed in Italy (0-0) to get to the finals. Hoddle; England's coach thought Gascoigne too much of a bad influence, and not fit enough to contribute. When he told Gazza the bad news, he apparently trashed the room in a rage of anger.

V
Van der Elst of Belgium was the oldest captain in the finals at 37 years of age; Belgium also had the oldest squad.

W
World Cup 98 a video game for multiple consoles was given the go ahead by FIFA in 1997, this was the first international football game from EA sports, and launched a phenomenon in gaming bringing the WORLD CUP to another stage.

X
Final XI: France: Barthez, Thuram, Lizarazu, Leboeuf, Desailly, Deschamps (c), Karembeu (Boghossian 57), Djorkaeff (Vieira 74), Guivarch (Dugarry 66), **Zidane (27,45), Petit (90)**

Brazil: Taffarel, Cafu, Aldair, Junior Baiano, César Sampaio (Edmundo 73), Roberto Carlos, Dunga (c), Ronaldo, Rivaldo, Leonardo (Denilson 46HT), Bebeto

Y
The Romanian team all bleached their hair **yellow** for their game v Tunisia in their last group game. They won the group and lost to Croatia in the next round.

Z
Zinedine Zidane got sent off in their 2nd game v Saudi Arabia and got 2 headed goals in the final beating Brazil 3-0, first brace of goals in a final since 1978.

WORLD CUP 2002

BRAZIL V GERMANY
2-0

FIFA World Cup A-Z of Facts and Figures

TEAM	STANDING	P	W	D	L	F-A
BRAZIL	CHAMPS	7	7	0	0	18-4
GERMANY	RU	7	5	1	1	14-3
TURKEY	SF	7	4	1	2	10-6
SOUTH KOREA	SF	7	3	2	2	8-6
SPAIN	QF	5	3	2	0	10-5
ENGLAND	QF	5	2	2	1	6-3
SENEGAL	QF	5	2	2	1	7-6
USA	QF	5	2	1	2	7-7
JAPAN	R2	4	2	1	1	5-3
DENMARK	R2	4	2	1	1	5-5
MEXICO	R2	4	2	1	1	4-4
REP OF IRELAND	R2	4	1	3	0	6-3
SWEDEN	R2	4	1	2	1	5-5
BELGIUM	R2	4	1	2	1	6-7
ITALY	R2	4	1	1	2	5-5
PARAGUAY	R2	4	1	1	2	6-7
SOUTH AFRICA	R1	3	1	1	1	5-5
ARGENTINA	R1	3	1	1	1	2-2
COSTA RICA	R1	3	1	1	1	5-6
CAMEROON	R1	3	1	1	1	2-3

FIFA World Cup A-Z of Facts and Figures

PORTUGAL	R1	3	1	0	2	6-4
RUSSIA	R1	3	1	0	2	4-4
CROATIA	R1	3	1	0	2	2-3
ECUADOR	R1	3	1	0	2	2-4
POLAND	R1	3	1	0	2	3-7
URUGUAY	R1	3	0	2	1	4-5
NIGERIA	R1	3	0	1	2	1-3
FRANCE	R1	3	0	1	2	0-3
TUNISIA	R1	3	0	1	2	1-5
SLOVENIA	R1	3	0	0	3	2-7
CHINA	R1	3	0	0	3	0-9
SAUDI ARABIA	R1	3	0	0	3	0-12

FIFA World Cup A-Z of Facts and Figures

A
Argentina who was pre-tournament favourites was knocked out in the group stages, by only drawing their last game v Sweden. They lost to England and a vengeful David Beckham after 1998, and Beckham dually scored the penalty that beat them 1-0. Canniga was sent off from the bench in the game v Sweden.

B
Brazil became winners for the 5th time, struggled in qualifying, but apart from the game v England sailed to the final with some great displays. Brazil beat Germany 2-0 in the final, which unbelievably is the first time these two great WORLD CUP teams have met in the WORLD CUPs history. Cafu was playing in his 3rd consecutive WORLD CUP final. Also went 7 games unbeaten in the tournament, both records. Top scorers in WORLD CUP with 18 goals.

C
Cautioned for a bad tackle in the Semi-final saw Germany's Michael Ballack miss the final. He went on to score the winning goal v South Korea (1-0) that saw the Germans reach their 7th final (also Brazil's 7th final). Most cautions to date, in a WORLD CUP finals match was between Cameroon and Germany with 8 cautions each.

D
Debutants Senegal proved worth qualifiers and progressed out of a tough group by beating France in their first game 1-0 and draws v Denmark and Uruguay saw them through. The 3-33 v Denmark saw the best comeback ever in WORLD CUP history from Uruguay being 3-0 down. A golden goal v Sweden saw them into the Quarters, but they fell to a golden goal v Turkey.

E
England was coached by Swede Sven-Goran Eriksson; their first foreign coach and made it to the Quarter final. 2 draws and a win saw them through the groups, and a convincing 3-0-win v Denmark next, saw them play Brazil in the Quarters. Taking the lead through Owen, this seemed to jump Brazil into action, and they were soon level, and after a freakish cross come goal from Ronaldinho England were 2-1

down. Against 10 men for the last 30 minutes, after Ronaldinho got sent off, England didn't go for the jugular, and were out. All of England's goals in third WORLD CUP were scored in the first half.

F
Holders **France** were knocked out in the group stages without scoring a goal, first time previous winners in a WORLD CUP have not reached the next round. Henry got sent off v Uruguay in the second group game after 25 minutes, restricting France's goal threat, they drew 0-0.

G
Germany who was beaten 5-1 at home v England in the qualifiers made the final. They beat Saudi Arabia 8-0 in the group stage (keeper Al-Deayea conceded 12 in 3 games, and a joint record 25 in finals appearances, with Carbajal of Mexico), their biggest WORLD CUP win to date. They then won their entire knock out games up to the final 1-0, with German resilience.

H
Hakan Suker scored the fastest WORLD CUP goal ever, to date, in the 3rd place game v South Korea after 11 seconds, Turkey went on to win the game 3-2, in a fast-paced quality game.

I
Rep of **Ireland** got out of their group for their 3rd WORLD CUP in a row, but lost to Spain on penalties 3-2, in a tense last 16 game. Robbie Keane's late equaliser v Germany in the group game saw him be the only player apart from Ronaldo to score against Germany in this WORLD CUP.

J
Japan topped their group after wins v Tunisia and Russia and draw v Belgium. They succumb to Turkey in the next round, but should be proud of their efforts, and the amazing support of their boisterous fans.

FIFA World Cup A-Z of Facts and Figures

K
Roy **Keane** captain of Ireland departed before a ball was kicked, due to falling out with coach McCarthy over the unprofessional Irish setup and lack of good training facilities. Sorely missed.

L
Luciano Gaucci Perugia's president said after Italy was controversially knocked out by South Korea that Perugia's Korean Ahn Jung-hwan scorer of the winner v Italy would never play for them again. He retracted these 24 hours later.

M
The **metatarsal** bone broken by David Beckham weeks before the WORLD CUP, became the biggest news build up in England, he just made it, but was not fully fit, and still had concerns about his foot, which was maybe why he jumped out of a tackle he would have normally made in their Quarter final v Brazil, which led to Brazil's first goal?

N
The **Netherlands** who got to the Semi's in 1998, failed to qualify, after losing to Portugal and Ireland and finishing 3rd in their group.

O
Out of the WORLD CUP on penalties, Spain; the big under achievers felt cheated in their defeat v South Korea in the Quarters. They had 2 goals disallowed; hit the post, before eventually losing 5-3 on penalties after a 0-0 draw.

P
Portugal's golden generation were eliminated in a group they were favourites to win. They lost v USA 3-2, beat Poland 4-0 (Pauleta 3), before losing to South Korea 1-0, and were knocked out.

Q
Qualifying consisted of 198 nations; a record. South Korea qualified for the 5th finals in succession, the first Asian nation to do this. Australia beat American Samoa 31-0, with Archie Thompson scoring

13; both records. Australia were eventually knocked out v Uruguay in a playoff. Rep of Ire qualified via a playoff v Iran over 2 legs 2-0, 0-1. The game in Iran had a crowd of 119,000 fans. The youngest player to play in a qualifying match is Souleymane Mamam of Togo v Zambia aged 13 years, 10 months and 6 days. Larrson (Sweden) and Turkyilmaz (Swiss) both scored hatricks from the penalty spots in qualifying.

R
Ronaldo of Brazil was WORLD CUP top scorer with 8 goals, first time over 6 goals since 1974. He eventually exorcised his demons of 4 years earlier, by scoring 2 in the final.

S
South Korea finally got their first WORLD CUP finals win, which came against Poland 2-0. Dutch coach Hiddink (in his second successive semi) played fast, attacking football and with supreme fitness, they reached the semi-finals. They beat Italy 2-1 on a golden goal in a controversial game, that saw some strange refereeing decisions going against the Italians, and Totti getting sent off for diving. A lot of luck v Spain next, saw them eventually finish in 4th place; best finish for an Asian nation.

T
Turkey made it to the semi-finals, and there best ever finish (3rd), in a WORLD CUP to date. They got through the group stage, runners up to Brazil, who they met again in the semi losing 1-0. Ilhan of Turkey scored the last golden goal of the WORLD CUP v Senegal; it was scrapped after the tournament.

U
Hakan **Unsal** of Turkey got sent off in the group game v Brazil for an aimless soft kick of the ball at Rivaldo, in added time, which hit him in the midrift, but Rivaldo faked embarrassingly that it hit him in the face. Rivaldo scored the winner 3 minutes from time from the penalty spot.

FIFA World Cup A-Z of Facts and Figures

V
Venues of the finals were for the first time in Asia, as South Korea and Japan co-hosted (a first) the WORLD CUP finals. They both had the majority newly built stadiums for the finals, and each provided 10 venues.

W
World Cup firsts as teams from Europe, N and S America, Asia and Africa had a team in the Quarter finals.

X
Final XI: Brazil: Marcos, Edmilson, Lucio, Roque Junior, Cafu (c), Kleberson, Gilberto, Roberto Carlos, Ronaldinho (Juninho Paulesta 85), Rivaldo, **Ronaldo (67,79)** (Denilson 90)
 Germany: Kahn (c), Linke, Ramelow, Metzelder, Frings, Schneider, Jeremies (Asamoah 77), Hamann, Bode (Ziege), Neuville) Klose (Bierhoff 74)

Y
Yokohoma stadium in Japan was the venue of the final, 70,000 capacity, and the biggest in Japan.

Z
Zinedine Zidane's only appearance in this WORLD CUP because of injury was in the 3rd game v Denmark which France lost 2-0.

123

WORLD CUP 2006

ITALY V FRANCE
1-1 (5-3 PENS)

FIFA World Cup A-Z of Facts and Figures

	STANDING	P	W	D	L	F-A
ITALY	CHAMPS	7	5	2	0	12-2
FRANCE	RU	7	4	3	0	9-3
GERMANY	SF	7	5	1	1	14-6
PORTUGAL	SF	7	4	1	2	7-5
BRAZIL	QF	5	4	0	1	10-2
ARGENTINA	QF	5	3	2	0	11-3
ENGLAND	QF	5	3	2	0	6-2
UKRAINE	QF	5	2	1	2	5-7
SPAIN	R2	4	3	0	1	9-4
SWITZERLAND	R2	4	2	2	0	4-0
NETHERLANDS	R2	4	2	1	1	3-2
ECUADOR	R2	4	2	0	2	5-4
GHANA	R2	4	2	0	2	4-6
SWEDEN	R2	4	1	2	1	3-4
MEXICO	R2	4	1	1	2	5-5
AUSTRALIA	R2	4	1	1	2	5-6
SOUTH KOREA	R1	3	1	1	1	3-4
PARAGUAY	R1	3	1	0	2	2-2
IVORY COAST	R1	3	1	0	2	5-6
CZECH REPUBLIC	R1	3	1	0	2	3-4

FIFA World Cup A-Z of Facts and Figures

POLAND	R1	3	1	0	2	2-4
CROATIA	R1	3	0	2	1	2-3
ANGOLA	R1	3	0	2	1	1-2
TUNISIA	R1	3	0	1	2	3-6
IRAN	R1	3	0	1	2	2-6
USA	R1	3	0	1	2	2-6
TRINIDAD & TOBAGO	R1	3	0	1	2	0-4
TOGO	R1	3	0	0	3	1-6
COSTA RICA	R1	3	0	0	3	3-9
SERBIA & MONTENEGRO	R1	3	0	0	3	2-10

FIFA World Cup A-Z of Facts and Figures

A
Australia qualified via a playoff v Uruguay 0-1, 1-0, and then winning 4-2 on penalties in front of 83,000 in Australia. They beat Japan with 3 goals in the last 10 minutes seeing them win a group game, and through to the next round; the first Oceania team to do get out of their group. They fell at the next hurdle to Italy getting beat 1-0, 5 minutes into stoppage time to a dubious penalty scored by Totti.

B
Brazil won all their group games, then beat Ghana, they eventually got knocked out in the Quarter finals by France 1-0, Brazils first WORLD CUP finals defeat since the final in 1998 (also v France).

C
Esteban **Cambiasso** of Argentina scored the goal of the tournament v Serbia and Montenegro, after 24 passes throughout the team they cruised to a 6-0 win. They lost in the Quarters v Germany on penalties 4-2 after 1-1 draw. Cambiasso missed the crucial penalty. Argentina's first defeat in a penalty shootout, Germans still not lost one.

D
A **defender** scored the first and last goal of the tournament, a first in any previous WORLD CUP. Lahm (Germany), and Matterazi (Italy).

E
England topped their group, which set up a last 16 game v Ecuador, which England clung on to win 1-0. Next was Portugal, who like in Euro 2004 put England out on penalties. Wayne Rooney got sent off, for an alleged stamp on Carvalho, after 0-0 score line, England lost 3-1 on penalties.

F
Luis **Figo** Portugal's talisman for so many years made his final appearance in the 3rd place playoff v Germany, losing 3-1, he set up his nation's goal.

G
Fabio **Grosso** of Italy scored a 118th minute goal in the semi-final v Germany to help his team to the final, they finally won 2-0. He also scored the winning penalty in the shootout in the final. Italy's first finals win on penalties, and they won scoring all of theirs (5-3)

H
There were no **hat-tricks** in this WORLD CUP, a first for a finals.

I
Italy won their 4th WORLD CUP, due to a solid defence and solidarity. The only goals they conceded were a penalty and an own goal. Like 1982 build up for the Azzuri, there was talks of match fixing back home, which bought the team togetherness. 21 out of 23-man squad was used. No player scored more than 2 goals and had 10 different scorers equalling France in 1982.

J
San **Juan** de Tibas, San **Jose** has the distinction of being the place where the lowest attendance to a WORLD CUP qualifying game when 0 people watched Costa Rica v Panama. Costa Rica fans were banned due to previous fans violence.

K
Jürgen Klinsmann's Germany finished in 3rd place in their own WORLD CUP. They had a young, fresh, attacking team that played high tempo football. They were the tournament's top scorers with 14 goals. Klose was the top scorer of the tournament with 5 goals, the lowest since 1962.

L
Luiz Filipe Scolari Brazilian winning coach 4 years earlier, coached Portugal to 4th place, and Portugal's first semi-final since 1966. It was Scolari's 3rd successive tournament Quarter final defeat of Erickson's England.

FIFA World Cup A-Z of Facts and Figures

M
Motto of the tournament 'A time to make friends', which was aptly named due to the generosity and welcoming nature of the German people, and atmosphere at fan festivals.

N
'The Battle of **Nuremburg**' was a last 16 game between Portugal and Holland, which Portugal won 1-0, but not after referee Ivanov issuing 4 red cards and 16 yellow; a record for a finals game to date. 2 reds for each side, and 9 yellows to Portugal and 7 to Holland.

O
Opening match of the tournament saw Germany beat Costa Rica 4-2, this is the highest scoring opening match in the final's history. Also, the first time the holders didn't open the tournament.

P
Graham **Poll** England's refereeing representative infamously goes down as the only referee to give the same player 3 red cards (SImunic of Croatia), v Australia. He had already sent off two players but failed to send off Simunic for a second yellow card, he eventually sent him off for dissent at the end of the game. The referee said he put Simunic's number down, but in the wrong column; against Australia's Craig Moore.

Q
Qualifying consisted of 194 entrants. Debutants were Trinidad and Tobago, Serbia and Montenegro, Togo, Angola, Ivory Coast, Ghana, Czech Rep and Ukraine. Trinidad and Tobago (the smallest nation by population to qualify for the WORLD CUP), qualified with the help and a goal from their only ever white player Chris Birchall v Bahrain

R
Ronaldo of Brazil became the top scorer in WORLD CUP finals history with 15 goals, with a goal v Ghana in the last 16.

S
Semi-finals were represented by just teams from Europe; Germany, Italy, Portugal and France, this is the 4th time this happened with 1934, 1966 and 1982 being the others.

T
The **tournament's** first ever game where a game was won by the opposition scoring an own goal was in the England v Paraguay game. Carlos Gamarra being the unlucky man.

U
Ukraine got to the Quarter finals in their debut WORLD CUP, since splitting from USSR. They came 2nd in their group, and played Switzerland next, and beat them on penalties 3-0, after drawing 0-0. Switzerland became the first team to not score a penalty in a shootout, and without conceding a goal in the tournament. Ukraine's luck ran out in the next round losing 3-0 to Italy.

V
Venues for the finals were played over 12 grounds, with the final being played at Berlin's Olympic Stadium. Many was known during the tournament under different names due to them not being FIFA sponsors, so the Allianz Arena was renamed the 'FIFA World Cup Stadium Munich for the tournament.

W
WAGS-Wives and Girlfriends became a popular phrase during the WORLD CUP. Eriksson decided to let them stay in the same German Spa as the players, was this a distraction? The Germans did the same!!

X
Final XI: Italy: Buffon, Grosso, Cannavaro (c), Gattuso, Totti (De Rossi 61), Cameronesi (Del Piero 86), Zambrotta, Perrota (Iaquinta 61), Pirlo, **Matterazi (19)**

France: Barthez, Abidal, Vieira (Diarra 56), Gallas, Makelele, Malouda, **Zidane (7 p),** Henry (Wiltord 107), Thuram, Sagnol, Ribery (Trezeguet 100)

Y

12 yards seems to be topical during this WORLD CUP. Ricardo of Portugal saved 3 spot kicks in a shootout, a record. Also, after the shootout between Argentina and Germany, Argentina's Cuffre was sent off for kicking Mertesaker. Latest ever sending off in a finals game. Trezeguet of France missed the vital and only penalty in The Final shootout.

Z

Zinedine Zidane was sent off in his final game as a player for head-butting Matterazi in the mid-rift. Earlier in the game he deliciously chipped Buffon with a penalty. Even after this controversy he was awarded the player of the tournament.

WORLD CUP 2010

SPAIN V NETHERLANDS
1-0

FIFA World Cup A-Z of Facts and Figures

TEAM	STANDING	P	W	D	L	F-A
SPAIN	CHAMPS	7	6	0	1	8-2
NETHERLANDS	RU	7	6	0	1	12-6
GERMANY	RU	7	5	0	2	16-5
URUGUAY	SF	7	3	2	2	11-8
ARGENTINA	QF	5	4	0	1	10-6
BRAZIL	QF	5	3	1	1	9-4
GHANA	QF	5	2	2	1	5-4
PARAGUAY	QF	5	1	3	1	3-2
JAPAN	R2	4	2	1	1	4-2
CHILE	R2	4	2	0	2	3-5
PORTUGAL	R2	4	1	2	1	7-1
USA	R2	4	1	2	1	5-5
ENGLAND	R2	4	1	2	1	3-5
MEXICO	R2	4	1	1	2	4-5
SOUTH KOREA	R2	4	1	1	2	6-8
SLOVAKIA	R2	4	1	1	2	5-7
IVORY COAST	R1	3	1	1	1	4-3
SLOVENIA	R1	3	1	1	1	3-3
SWITZERLAND	R1	3	1	1	1	1-1
SOUTH AFRICA	R1	3	1	1	1	3-5
AUSTRALIA	R1	3	1	1	1	3-6
NEW ZEALAND	R1	3	0	3	0	2-2
SERBIA	R1	3	1	0	2	2-3

FIFA World Cup A-Z of Facts and Figures

DENMARK	R1	3	1	0	2	3-6
GREECE	R1	3	1	0	2	2-5
ITALY	R1	3	0	2	1	4-5
NIGERIA	R1	3	0	1	2	3-5
ALGERIA	R1	3	0	1	2	0-2
FRANCE	R1	3	0	1	2	1-4
HONDURUS	R1	3	0	1	2	0-3
CAMEROON	R1	3	0	0	3	2-5
NORTH KOREA	R1	3	0	0	3	1-12

FIFA World Cup A-Z of Facts and Figures

A

South **Africa** hosted the first WORLD CUP in Africa; the bidding process for hosting the WORLD CUP was only open for African nations. Morocco and Egypt were the other candidates, but South Africa won the vote in the end. They were the first host nation not to qualify from their group, having drawn their first game, lost second, but beat France 2-1 in the last game. They went out on goal difference to Mexico.

B

'**Black Stars**' Ghana was the only African nation to get through the group round, and so nearly made the semi-finals. They beat the USA in last 16, in extra time 2-1, this set up the Quarter final v Uruguay which finished 1-1 after extra time, but if Gyan had scored a last-minute penalty for deliberate handball by Suárez, they would have been semi-finalists. It went to penalties, and all though Gyan scored this time, they lost 4-2.

C

Carlos Alberto Perreira became the first coach to manage 6 nations at WORLD CUP's; Kuwait 82, UAE 90, Brazil 94&06, Saudi Arabia 98 and South Africa 2010. He also has lost the most matches jointly with Milutonivic with 9.

D

Dunga Brazil's captain and WORLD CUP winner in 94 coached Brazil to the Quarters. They topped the group, and then beat Chile in the next round 3-0. Holland came from behind to beat Brazil 2-1. This was Brazil's first loss outside of Europe in a finals match since 1950 Maracanazo game v Uruguay.

E

England scraped through their group with a last game struggle against Slovenia 1-0, Defoe the scorer. Finishing second meant a last 16 game v Germany. Germany beat the hapless English 4-1. At 1-1 Lampard hit a long-range effort at goal, which hit the underside of the bar, and went a couple of feet over the line, but the referee didn't give the goal. This was England's worst finals defeat.

F
First time all 5 CONMEBOL sides had progressed from group stages, four of the teams as winners; Uruguay semi-final, Argentina, Brazil and Paraguay the Quarters and Chile the last 16.

G
Germany were the WORLD CUP top scorers again with 16 goals and fell at the semi-final stage as they have in their last two tournaments (WORLD CUP 2006, Euro 2008). They beat Uruguay 3-2 in the 3rd place playoff. Germany hold the record for most 3rd place finishes (4), and Uruguay the most with 4th place finishes (3).

H
Howard Webb became the first Englishman since Jack Taylor in 1974 to referee a WORLD CUP final. In an ill-tempered game he had to hand out 14 yellow cards and 1 red (9 yellow and 1 red to the disgraceful Dutch), more than doubling the previous worst final in 1986, where 6 cards were given out. Heittenga became the 4th player sent off in a WORLD CUP final. He was the first referee to take charge of the Champions League Final and WORLD CUP Final in the same year.

I
Italy was knocked out in the group stages; they became the 3rd previous winners to be knocked out in the first round following Brazil 66 and France 2002. Also, France the beaten finalist last time got knocked out without winning a game in their group.

J
David **James**; England's keeper, became the oldest player to debut in a finals match at 39 years 10 months and 17 days v Algeria, and kept a clean sheet.

K
Korea had both North and South represented in the same WORLD CUP. North Korea who lost a group game v Portugal 7-0, didn't

progress. South Korea got to the last 16 before getting knocked out by Uruguay 2-1

L
Joachim **Loew**, steered Germany to their 3rd consecutive semi-final (he was assistant in 2006), narrowingly losing to Spain 1-0, as they did in Euro 2008 final.

M
Diego **Maradona** coached Argentina in his first coaching job since Racing Club in 1995. He kicked every ball, and played direct attacking football, which saw them, beat lesser teams easily enough, but become unstuck v Germany in the Quarters losing 4-0.

N
Netherlands lost their 3rd WORLD CUP final in 3 appearances in the final. van Marwjik had them playing some great flowing football leading up to the final, coming from behind to beat Brazil in the Quarters 2-1, and before losing in the final they were unbeaten in 25 matches and a 14-game winning streak.

O
Otto Rehhagel became the oldest person to coach a finals team when he took charge of Greece for their game v Argentina at 71 years, 10 months and 13 days.

P
Paul the German Octopus became a sensation during the finals, due to his accurate predictions on who would win games. He predicted all 7 of Germany's results, and Spain's win in the final, by choosing from two boxes with food in it put in his tank with each country national flag on each box. He sadly died in October 2010.

Q
Qualifying consisted of 204 out of 208 FIFA recognised nations, including for the second time the reigning champions Italy having to qualify (Brazil 2006 1st). Controversy engulfed the France v Rep Ireland playoff, when Henry of France scored the winning goal with a

deliberate handball and knocked out the Irish. Slovakia and Serbia qualified for the first time as independent countries. Slovakia got through the group with a last-minute goal to knock out the Italians.

R
Ravshan Irmatov became top appearance holder in games refereed in one final with 5 games; he jointly holds this record with Archundia (Mex) and Elizando (Arg) in 2006.

S
Spain the serial under achievers finally won their first WORLD CUP and became the 2nd team to hold both the Euro crown as well. They were the first European nation to win a WORLD CUP on a foreign continent, and it was 60 years since in last semi-final. Things started badly as Switzerland beat them in their opening game (first time the eventual winner has lost their first game and won tournament), but they rallied to win next two games, and finish top of the group. They beat Portugal, Paraguay and Germany in the knock out games all 1-0, and Holland in the final by the same score, becoming champions who scored the least amount of goals (Also only 3 different players scored all tournament; Villa, Puyol and Iniesta), but also only let in 2 goals all tournament. Iniesta scored the latest goal in a final to win a game from 0-0 in the 116th minute.

T
Top scorer of the WORLD CUP was shared between Muller (Ger), Sneidjer (Holl), Forlan (Uru) and Villa (Spa) with 5 goals.

U
Uruguay finished 4th and had to play 20 games to qualify, Forlan won the Golden Boot for his great displays.

V
Venues for the WORLD CUP had a lot of travelling, from Polokwane in the North to Cape Town in the South. 10 stadiums were used during the tournament, 5 were newly built, and 5 refurbished and modernized. The atmosphere at every game was amped up, mainly

due to the hum of vuvuzelas. The final was held in Soccer City, Johannesburg with a capacity of 84,500.

W

Brothers **Wilson**, Jerry and Johnny Palacios of Honduras; were in the same squad. Also, brothers Jerome and Kevin –Prince Boateng played against each other when Germany played Ghana.

X

Final XI: Spain: Casillas (c), Pique, Puyol, **Iniesta (116),** Villa (Torres 106), Xavi, Capdevilla, Alonso (Fabregas 87), Ramos, Busquets, Pedro (Navas 60)

Netherlands: Stekelenberg, van der Wiel, Heittenga, Mathjsen, van Bronckhurst (Braafheid 105), van Bommel, Kuyt (Elia 70), de Jong (van der Vaart 99), van Persie, Sneijder, Robben

Y

Mexico and England were **yearning** for new technology, after incidents hindered their progress in the competition. Mexico's case was a goal given offside, but seconds later the replay was shown on a big screen in the stadium showing the goal was legitimate, to the disgust of all watching. Blatter the FIFA president said that a meeting regarding these matters would be had to resolve matters.

Z

New **Zealand** was the only undefeated team in the tournament with three draws but was knocked out in the group stage.

WORLD CUP 2014

GERMANY V ARGENTINA
1-0

FIFA World Cup A-Z of Facts and Figures

TEAM	STANDING	P	W	D	L	F-A
GERMANY	CHAMPS	7	6	1	0	18-4
ARGENTINA	RU	7	5	1	1	8-4
NETHERLANDS	SF	7	5	2	0	15-4
BRAZIL	SF	7	3	2	2	11-14
COLOMBIA	QF	5	4	0	1	12-4
BELGIUM	QF	5	4	0	1	6-3
FRANCE	QF	5	3	1	1	10-3
COSTA RICA	QF	5	2	3	0	5-2
CHILE	R2	4	2	1	1	6-4
MEXICO	R2	4	2	1	1	5-3
SWITZERLAND	R2	4	2	0	2	7-7
URUGUAY	R2	4	2	0	2	4-6
GREECE	R2	4	1	2	1	3-5
ALGERIA	R2	4	1	1	2	7-7
USA	R2	4	1	1	2	5-6
NIGERIA	R2	4	1	1	2	3-5
ECUADOR	R1	3	1	1	1	3-3
PORTUGAL	R1	3	1	1	1	4-7
CROATIA	R1	3	1	0	2	6-6
BOSNIA HERZIGOVINA	R1	3	1	0	2	4-4
ITALY	R1	3	1	0	2	2-3
SPAIN	R1	3	1	0	2	4-7
RUSSIA	R1	3	0	2	1	2-3
GHANA	R1	3	0	1	2	4-6

FIFA World Cup A-Z of Facts and Figures

ENGLAND	R1	3	0	1	2	2-4
SOUTH KOREA	R1	3	0	1	2	3-6
IRAN	R1	3	0	1	2	1-4
JAPAN	R1	3	0	1	2	2-6
AUSTRALIA	R1	3	0	0	3	3-9
HONDURUS	R1	3	0	0	3	1-8
CAMEROON	R1	3	0	0	3	1-9

FIFA World Cup A-Z of Facts and Figures

A
Argentina led my Lionel Messi made it to their first final since 1990 and against Germany for the 3rd time. They won all their group games, and then beat a spirited Swiss team and pre-tournament favourites Belgium 1-0. Argentina beat the Netherlands 4-2 on penalties after 0-0 draw, this saw Argentina become joint top with Germany for most wins in shootouts in finals history with 4, and most overall with 5. The Netherlands lost their 2nd semi-final shootout.

B
Brazil hosted their 2nd WORLD CUP and 20th in all (every WORLD CUP to date) and tried to lay the ghost of the Maracanazo of 1950, a massive weight was on all associated with the squad; the expectation to win was gigantic. They played well enough to get out of the group (as they have in every WORLD CUP) but stumbled over the line v Chile on penalties 3-2, then in the Quarters just beat Colombia 2-1, being outplayed in both games. Neymar was their only shining light but got injured for the semi-final…. how they needed him. They embarrassingly got beat 7-1 v Germany, with 5 goals in 5 crazy minutes. Their worst defeat ever in the finals. Scolari; coach of 2002 winners were coach again but resigned soon after.

C
Colombia was a surprise seeded team for the tournament, even after missing the last 4 tournaments, won all their group games scoring 9 goals. Top scorer of WORLD CUP was James Rodriguez with 6.

D
Draws were scarce in the group stages only 8 in total, the first coming in the 13th game Iran v Nigeria 0-0. In all 136 goals were scored in the group stage the largest since 32 team format.

E
England failed to win any group games, drew last game v Costa Rica, but already out. This was there worse showing since 1958, and first time they had lost both opening games.

F
Les **Fennecs** (Algeria) became the first African nation to score 4 goals in a match (v South Korea), also first time two African nations got out of their groups, as Nigeria did as well. Algeria held Germany to a 0-0 draw in the last 16, eventually going down 2-1 with late goals (92,120 for Germany, 121 for Algeria).

G
This WORLD CUP had the most **goals** scored, jointly with 1998 WORLD CUP with 171 goals, also had the most individual scorers with 121 goals.

H
Tim **Howard** the keeper of USA saved a record 16 shots in the game v Belgium, USA eventually lost 2-1 in extra time, after 0-0 in normal time.

I
Ivory Coast, who boasted Africa's best players, fell at the group stage for the 3rd tournament running. Star player Drogba, retired after the WORLD CUP.

J
Against **Japan**; Faryd Mondragon, Colombia's keeper became the oldest player to play in the finals to date, at 43 years and 3 days old, his last appearance at the finals was 16 years earlier, making this the biggest gap since finals games. Oldest player ever in qualifying was MacDonald Taylor for US Virgin Islands v St Kitts and Nevis aged 46 years 5 months and 22 days.

K
Christoph **Kramer** of Germany started the WORLD CUP Final, after only one previous substitute appearance in these finals lasting 11 minutes. During the warmup Khedeira got injured, so he got his chance, but Kramer had to be substituted himself in the first half due to a head injury. He asked the referee if he was playing in the WORLD CUP Final, so the ref informed Schweinsteiger to get him subbed.

FIFA World Cup A-Z of Facts and Figures

L
Luis Suarez Uruguay striker got banned for 9 games after biting Chiellini of Italy on the shoulder in their group game. Suarez had previously got banned for doing this at his club Liverpool a few months earlier.

M
Miroslav Klose became the WORLD CUP leading goal scorer of all time with his goal v Brazil taking his tally to 16. He has also played the most knock out games (17), most matches won (17). 12 years between first and last goals, and first player to play in 4 WORLD CUP semi-finals.

N
Netherlands played some scintillating group stage football beating defending champions in a repeat of the final of 2010 5-1 in their opening game. They won all 3 group games. During the last 16 game v Mexico, the WORLD CUP had its first ever cooling break, which came in the 32nd minute; they won on penalties v Costa Rica in the Quarters after 0-0 draw but succumb to Argentina on penalties in the semi. They convincingly beat a disappointing Brazil in the 3rd place playoff 3-0.

O
'Ole Ola' was the official song of the finals meaning 'We are One', and was sung by Pitbull, Jennifer Lopez and Claudia Leitte, very unforgettable.

P
Protests prior to the WORLD CUP took place, organized by people unhappy with the amount of public money spent on the WORLD CUP. Blatter was booed during the Confederations Cup a year earlier, so no speeches were made during the opening ceremony.

Q
207 teams took part. In **qualifying** Luxemburg failed to qualify for their 19th WORLD CUP in succession. Bosnia and Herzegovina

qualified for the first time. Australia qualified as part of the Asian pool section; Uruguay again qualified AS 5TH placed so went in playoff this time beating Jordon on aggregate.

R
Raphael Marquez became the player who was captain for four WORLD CUPs for Mexico from 2002-14, a record.

S
Spain became the first defending champions to be out after just 2 games, 1 week into the tournament.

T
New **technology** was finally utilized in this WORLD CUP. Goal line technology was bought in at last, with a camera on the line relayed to an official, first time used was an own goal by Noel Valledares from Honduras v France. Vanishing foam was used to mark free kick positioning.

U
Under dogs Costa Rica were the surprise team of the WORLD CUP, finishing top of their group, ahead of England, Uruguay and Italy. Won and lost on penalties in knock out rounds.

V
Some **venues** for the WORLD CUP were just completed before the tournament began, 7 were new, and 5 renovated. The completion was more spread out than 1950, with hours being spent in traveling. England played Italy in their opener in the rainforest venue of Manaus.

W
Some **venues** for the WORLD CUP were just completed before the tournament began, 7 were new, and 5 renovated. The completion was more spread out than 1950, with hours being spent in traveling. England played Italy in their opener in the rainforest venue of Manaus.

FIFA World Cup A-Z of Facts and Figures

X
Final XI: Germany: Neuer, Howedes, Hummels, Schweinsteiger, Ozil (Mertesaker 120), Klose (**Götze 88, (113))**, Muller, Lahm (c), Kroos, Boateng, Kramer (Schurrle 31)

Argentina: Romero, Garay, Zabaleta, Biglia, Pérez (Gago 86), Higuain (Palacio 78), Messi (c), Mascherano, Demicheles, Rojo, Lavezzi (Agüero 46 HT)

Y
12 **yards** out for a penalty shootout seemed too much for Holland keeper Cillesen as he was substituted with minutes to spare in the knockout game v Costa Rica. Cillesen had never saved a penalty before, so coach van Gaal substituted Cillesen, replacing him with Tim Krul because he was a better penalty saver), and it worked he saved 2 penalties. He didn't use this tactic in the semi-final though.

Z
Zuniga of Colombia put out poster boy and Brazilian saviour Neymar in their knockout game with a tackle from behind and breaking his back.

WORLD CUP 2018

FRANCE CROATIA
4-2

FIFA World Cup A-Z of Facts and Figures

TEAM	STANDING	P	W	D	L	F-A
FRANCE	CHAMPS	7	6	1	0	14-6
CROATIA	RU	7	4	2	1	14-9
BELGIUM	SF	7	6	0	1	16-6
ENGLAND	SF	7	3	1	3	12-8
URUGUAY	QF	5	4	0	1	7-3
BRAZIL	QF	5	3	1	1	8-3
SWEDEN	QF	5	3	0	2	6-4
RUSSIA	QF	5	2	2	1	11-7
COLOMBIA	R2	4	2	1	1	6-3
SPAIN	R2	4	1	3	0	7-6
DENMARK	R2	4	1	3	0	3-2
MEXICO	R2	4	2	0	2	3-6
PORTUGAL	R2	4	1	2	1	6-6
SWITZERLAND	R2	4	1	2	1	5-5
JAPAN	R2	4	1	1	2	6-7
ARGENTINA	R2	4	1	1	2	6-9
SENEGAL	R1	3	1	1	1	4-4
IRAN	R1	3	1	1	1	2-2
S KOREA	R1	3	1	0	2	3-3
PERU	R1	3	1	0	2	2-2
NIGERIA	R1	3	1	0	2	3-4
GERMANY	R1	3	1	0	2	2-4
SERBIA	R1	3	1	0	2	2-4
TUNISIA	R1	3	1	0	2	5-8
POLAND	R1	3	1	0	2	2-5
S ARABIA	R1	3	1	0	2	2-7

FIFA World Cup A-Z of Facts and Figures

MOROCCO	R1	3	0	1	2	2-4
ICELAND	R1	3	0	1	2	2-5
COSTA RICA	R1	3	0	1	2	2-5
AUSTRALIA	R1	3	0	1	2	2-5
EGYPT	R1	3	0	0	3	2-6
PANAMA	R1	3	0	0	3	2-11

FIFA World Cup A-Z of Facts and Figures

A
Argentina crept through the group stage with a goal 4 minutes from time v Nigeria in their last game, otherwise would have been out. They eventually lost in a classic last 16 game v France 4-3. Messi still not scored in a knockout game in the 4 World Cups he's played in, but became the only player to score in his teens, 20's and 30's.

B
Belgium were the top scorers in the tournament with 16 goals. They won their group winning all 3 games, but eventually lost out in the semi-finals v France 1-0. They finished 3rd in the tournament after beating England again.

C
Croatia reached their first World Cup final after beating England in the semi-final. They won their group, and was the team with the most attacks, and best defending stats in the tournament (352 attacks, 301 clearance's, tackles and saves.) Mandzukic is to date the only player to score an own goal in a World Cup Final. He also scored for Croatia.

D
Didier Deschamps became the 3rd player and coach to win the World Cup, he also captained the French to victory in 1998. Zagello and Beckenbauer being the others.

E
England managed their equal best finish on foreign soil (4th), after losing to Croatia 2-1aet in the Semi Final. They won their first ever World Cup penalty shoot-out v Colombia, in the last 16. Also recorded their biggest win at a World Cup beating Panama 6-1.

F
France won their second World Cup, beating Croatia 4-2, the highest scoring final since 1966. In the whole tournament they were only behind for 9 minutes (v Argentina.)

G
Germany the 2014 winners, came bottom of their group, losing 2 of their 3 games. First time this happened since 1938.

H
Hosts for the World Cup were Russia. The first World Cup in Eastern Europe, and the biggest country to stage the competition. There were 11 host cities across 4 time zones, and 12 venues. The final was held at the Luzhniki Stadium. The most expensive World Cup to date budget wise, with £1.2 million being spent on contracts to kill stray dogs before the tournament began.

I
Iceland qualified for their first ever tournament and are the smallest nation by population to ever qualify. They finished bottom of their group with 1-point v Argentina in their first game.

J
Japan qualified from their group on the fair play rule, as all their standings were the same as Senegal's. First time this has happened. They had fewer yellow cards. They also became the first Asian team to defeat a South American team in 16 attempts, when they beat Columbia 2-1 in their group game. Eventually lost to Belgium in the last 16 3-2, after being 2-0 up.

K
Harry **Kane** was the top scorer in the completion with 6 goals, first Englishman since Gary Lineker in 1986. All his goals came in the group stage. Also scored a hat trick v Panama.

L
Luka Modric of Croatia was named as the Player of the Tournament, for his silky skills and midfield playmaking role. He also later won the Ballon D'Or, breaking a run of Ronaldo and Messi that went back to 2008.

FIFA World Cup A-Z of Facts and Figures

M
Match ball for the World Cup was inspired by the 1970 ball The Telstar 18 by adidas. Two balls popped during the Australia v France game.

N
Neymar of Brazil was the most fouled, and the most diving player in the tournament. He is the scorer of the latest goal to be scored in regulation time, in the game v Costa Rica, when he scored in the 97th minute. Brazil got knocked out in the Quarter finals by Belgium 2-1.

O
Oldest player in World Cup history to date, when he played for Egypt v Saudi Arabia was Essem El-Hadary. He was 45 years and 161 days old. He was also eldest captain and debutant ever. He was older than the managers of Senegal, Serbia and Belgium. Oldest outfield player Raphael Marquez of Mexico played in his 5th finals, equalling Carbajal, Matthaus and Buffon.

P
Portugal's Ronaldo became the oldest player to score a hat trick in the World Cup in the game v Spain which ended 3-3. He has to date never scored in the knockout stages in 4 World Cups.

Q
Qualifying had some noticeable absentees in Italy, Holland and the USA. Italy's last missed tournament was 1958, they lost in a playoff to Sweden 1-0. First time ever that all eligible teams applied to enter the tournament.

R
Russia won 5-0 in their opening game v Saudi Arabia, second biggest opening win since 1934. They lost in the Quarters v Croatia on penalties, after beating Spain in the last 16, also on penalties.

S
Substitutions in extra time was for the first time each team could put on a 4th player. Daler Kuziaev of Russia was the first player to do this.

T
Twelve own goals were scored in this World Cup, the most ever, and double the then record of 1998. Overall there was 168 goals scored, at an average of 2.64 per game.

U
Uruguay's Oscar Taberez was the oldest coach at the World Cup to date, at 71 years of age. He took Uruguay to the Quarters, in his 4th World Cup. He stalks the side-lines using his walking stick, as he has a condition called chronic neuropathy.

V
VAR (Video Assisted Referee) is introduced in this World Cup. Diego Costa became the first player to score a goal based on a VAR decision v Portugal. Only 4 players sent off in the tournament, lowest since 1978. Griezmann of France became the first to score a penalty awarded by VAR v Australia.

W
FIFA **World Cup** has a new president in Gianni Infantino, a Swiss-Italian, who took over from Sepp Blatter after bribery charges.

X
Final XI France: Lloris, Pavard, Varane, Umtiti, **Pogba (59), Griezmann (p38)**, Giroud (Fekir), **Mbappe (65)**, Kante (Nzonzi), Matuidi (Tolisso), Hernandez
Croatia: Subasic, Vrsaljko, Strinic (Pjaca), **Perisic (28)**, Lovren, Rakatic, Modric, Brozovic, **Mandzukic (og18,69)**, Rebic (Kramaric), Vida

Y
The second **youngest** scorer of a Final goal since Pelé in 1958, was Mbappe of France he was still a teenager at 19 years old.

Z
Zabivaka was the mascot of the World Cup, voted by 1 million Russians. It was a wolf and means 'one who scores.

FIFA World Cup A-Z of Facts and Figures

Acknowledgements

This book could not have been written if it was not for my passion for the World Cup, and all the glorious rich history that comes with this fanfare of football extravaganza. I would like to thank my sons Jack and Harry for all their time and enthusiasm in helping me write this, my first book, one of the most rewarding and gratifying things I have had the pleasure in doing.

Finally, I would like to thank my wife Sarah, who apart from thinking I'm mad spending most of my spare time researching and writing this book, found time to support me in something I felt passionate about.

Bibliography

Freddi, Cris. The Complete Book of The World Cup, London, CollinsWillow 1998
Crouch, Terry. The World Cup: The Complete History, London, Aurum Press Ltd 2002
http://www.planetworldcup.com Jan Alsos 1998-2014
http:// www.topendsports.com Topend Sports Network 1997-2014

Printed in Great Britain
by Amazon